THE FINE GOLD OF NEWMAN

THE FINE GOLD OF NEWMAN

THE MACMILLAN COMPANY
NEW YORK · BOSTON · CHICAGO · DALLAS
ATLANTA · SAN FRANCISCO

MACMILLAN & CO., LIMITED
LONDON · BOMBAY · CALCUTTA
MELBOURNE

THE MACMILLAN COMPANY
OF CANADA, LIMITED
TORONTO

THE
FINE GOLD
of NEWMAN

COLLECTED FROM HIS WRITINGS

by

JOSEPH J. REILLY, Ph.D.

AUTHOR OF "LOWELL AS A CRITIC,"
"NEWMAN AS A MAN OF LETTERS,"
ETC.

NEW YORK
THE MACMILLAN COMPANY
1931

Printed in the United States of America by
THE FERRIS PRINTING COMPANY, NEW YORK

TO

DR. JAMES M. KIERAN
PRESIDENT OF HUNTER COLLEGE
A PIONEER IN THE NEWMAN CLUB MOVEMENT

FOREWORD

Newman is one of the four great "prophets" of nineteenth century English Literature and beyond any of the others he is significant for our generation. His interest in the human heart; his appreciation of the meaning of great movements; his unswerving belief in unchanging truths; his detestation of cowardice, moral compromises, pharisaism, and prejudice; his reasoned wisdom in higher education; his belief in the unseen realities as the only abiding realities; his conviction that duty is personal, not vicarious; his poetic imagination; his own spiritual odyssey revealed in one of the world's greatest autobiographies; and, finally, his unerring sense of all that is exquisite in style have combined to keep Newman where his own contemporaries placed him—among English masters of the written word and the great spiritual leaders of the race.

Ours is a hurried generation, threatened with the loss of the art of reading with one's mind. It accepts Newman as a great man but confines its attention to three or four of his many volumes, and ignores the wisdom and beauty of the others. This book aims to offer from every phase of Newman's many-sided writings some of his noblest, wisest, and most perfect utterances. The man who wrote them has uncounted more which await the reader with the seeing eye and the understanding heart.

To the Reverend John W. Keogh of Philadelphia, Chaplain of the National Federation of Newman Clubs, my thanks are due and sincerely offered. It was he who first suggested the making of this selection of the *Fine Gold of Newman*.

J. J. R.

Hunter College, New York City
   April 6, 1931

ABBREVIATIONS OF WORKS FROM WHICH SELECTIONS HAVE BEEN TAKEN

A. D.	DIFFICULTIES OF ANGLICANS (2 vols.)
APOL.	APOLOGIA (Oxford Edition) *
CAL.	CALLISTA
D. and A.	DISCUSSIONS AND ARGUMENTS
D. CH. D.	DEVELOPMENT OF CHRISTIAN DOCTRINE
D. M. C.	DISCOURSES TO MIXED CONGREGATIONS
E. C. and H.	ESSAYS CRITICAL AND HISTORICAL (2 vols.)
G. of A.	GRAMMAR OF ASSENT
H. S.	HISTORICAL SKETCHES (3 vols.)
I. of U.	IDEA OF A UNIVERSITY
L. G.	LOSS AND GAIN
LET.	LETTERS (2 vols.)
L. J.	LECTURES ON JUSTIFICATION
O. U. S.	OXFORD UNIVERSITY SERMONS
P. P. C.	PRESENT POSITION OF CATHOLICS
P. P. S.	PAROCHIAL AND PLAIN SERMONS (8 vols.)
S. S. D.	SERMONS ON SUBJECTS OF THE DAY
S. V. O.	SERMONS ON VARIOUS OCCASIONS
WARD	CARDINAL NEWMAN (2 vols.) BY WILFRID WARD

* References to the APOLOGIA are to the edition edited by the late Wilfrid Ward and published by the Oxford University Press. All other references are to the regular edition published by Longmans, Green and Co., whom I hereby thank for their kindness in permitting me to print the selections in this volume.

THE FINE GOLD OF NEWMAN

THE FINE GOLD OF NEWMAN

THIS is the great, manifest, historical phenomenon which converted me,—to which all particular inquiries converged: Christianity is not a matter of opinion, but an external fact, entering into, carried out in, indivisible from, the history of the world. It has a bodily occupation of the world; it is one continuous fact or thing, the same from first to last, distinct from everything else: to be a Christian is to partake of, to submit to, this thing; and the simple question was, Where, what is this thing in this age, which in the first age was the Catholic Church? The answer was undeniable; the Church called Catholic now, is that very same thing in hereditary descent, in organization, in principles, in position, in external relations, which was called the Catholic Church then; name and thing have ever gone together, by an uninterrupted connection and succession, from then till now. (*A. D.* i. 368)

I AM as little hostile to physical science as I am to poetry or metaphysics; but I wish for studies of every kind a legitimate application: nor do I grudge them to anti-Catholics, so that anti-Catholics will not claim to monopolize them, cry out when we profess them, or direct them against Revelation.

I wish, indeed, I could think that these studies were not intended by a certain school of philosophers to bear directly against its authority. There are those who hope, there are those who are sure, that in the incessant investigation of facts, physical, political, and moral, something or other, or many things, will sooner or later turn up, and stubborn facts too, simply contradictory of revealed declarations. A vision comes before them of some physical or historical proof that mankind is not descended from a common origin, or that the hopes of the world were never consigned to a wooden ark floating on the waters, or that the manifestations on Mount Sinai were the work of man or nature, or that the Hebrew patriarchs or the judges of Israel are mythical personages, or that St. Peter had no connection with Rome, or that the doctrine of the Holy Trinity or of the Real Presence was foreign to primitive belief. An anticipation possesses them that the ultimate truths embodied in mesmerism will certainly solve all the Gospel miracles; or that to Niebuhrize the Gospels or the Fathers is a simple expedient for stultifying the whole Catholic system. They imagine that the eternal, immutable word of God is to quail and come to nought before the penetrating intellect of man. (*I. of U.*, p. 398f.)

MUTUAL education, in a large sense of the word, is one of the great and incessant occupations of human society, carried on partly with set purpose, and partly not. One generation forms another; and the existing generation is ever acting and reacting upon itself in the persons of its individual members. (*H. S.* III. 6f.)

WE have sermons in stones, and books in the running brooks; works, larger and more comprehensive than those which have gained for ancients an immortality, issue forth every morning, and are projected onwards to the ends of the earth at the rate of hundreds of miles a day. Our seats are strewed, our pavements are powdered, with swarms of little tracts; and the very bricks of our city walls preach wisdom, by informing us by their placards where we can at once cheaply purchase it.

Nevertheless, after all, even in this age, whenever men are really serious about getting what, in the language of trade, is called "a good article," when they aim at something precise, something refined, something really luminous, something really large, something choice, they go to another market; they avail themselves, in some shape or other, of the rival method, the ancient method, of oral instruction, of present communication between man and man, of teachers instead of learning, of the personal influence of a master, and the humble initiation of a disciple, and, in consequence, of great centres of pilgrimage and throng, which such a method of education necessarily involves. (*H. S.* III. 7)

TILL we have discovered some intellectual daguerreotype, which takes off the course of thought, and the form, lineaments, and features of truth, as completely and minutely as the optical instrument reproduces the sensible object, we must come to the teachers of wisdom to learn wisdom, we must repair to the fountain and drink there. Portions of it may go from thence to the ends of the earth by means of books; but the fulness is in one place alone. It is in such assemblages and congregations of intellect that books themselves, the masterpieces of human genius, are written, or at least originated. (*H. S.* III. 8)

IT IS the living voice, the breathing form, the expressive countenance, which preaches, which catechises. Truth, a subtle, invisible, manifold spirit, is poured into the mind of the scholar by his eyes and ears through his affections, imagination and reason; it is poured into his mind and is sealed up there in perpetuity, by propounding and repeating it, by questioning and requestioning, by correcting and explaining, by progressing and then recurring to first principles, by all those ways which are implied in the word "catechising." (*H. S.* III. 14)

A UNIVERSITY is a place of concourse, whither students come from every quarter for every kind of knowledge. You cannot have the best of every kind everywhere; you must go to some great city or emporium for it. There you have all the choicest productions of nature and art all together, which you find each in its own separate place elsewhere. All the riches of the land and of the earth are carried up thither; there are the best markets, and there the best workmen. It is the centre of trade, the supreme court of fashion, the umpire of rival talents, and the standard of things rare and precious. It is the place for seeing galleries of first-rate pictures, and for hearing wonderful voices and performers of transcendent skill. It is the place for great preachers, great orators, great nobles, great statesmen. It is the place to which a thousand schools make contributions; in which the intellect may safely range and speculate, sure to find its equal in some antagonist activity, and its judge in the tribunal of truth. It is a place where inquiry is pushed forward, and discoveries verified and perfected, and rashness rendered innocuous, and error exposed, by the collision of mind with mind and knowledge with knowledge. It is the place where the professor becomes eloquent and is a missionary and a preacher, displaying his science in its most complete and most winning form, pouring it forth with the zeal of enthusiasm, and lighting up his own love of it in

the breasts of his hearers. It is the place where the
catechist makes good his ground as he goes, treading in
the truth day by day into the ready memory, and wedg-
ing and tightening it into the expanding reason. It is
a place which wins the admiration of the young by its
celebrity, kindles the affections of the middle-aged by
its beauty, and rivets the fidelity of the old by its associations. It is a seat of wisdom, a light of the world, a
minister of the faith, an Alma Mater of the rising generation. (*H. S.* III. 15f.)

TO ATHENS, as a sort of ideal land, where all arche-
types of the great and the fair were found in substantial
being, and all departments of truth explored, and all
diversities of intellectual power exhibited, where taste
and philosophy were majestically enthroned as in a royal
court, where there was no sovereignty but that of mind,
and no nobility but that of genius, where professors
were rulers, and princes did homage, hither flocked continually from the very corners of the *orbis terrarum,* the
many-tongued generation, just rising, or just risen into
manhood, in order to gain wisdom. (*H. S.* III. 18)

PERICLES, who succeeded Cimon both in the government and in the patronage of art, is said by Plutarch
to have entertained the idea of making Athens the capital of federated Greece: in this he failed, but his en-
couragement of such men as Phidias and Anaxagoras led
the way to her acquiring a far more lasting sovereignty
over a far wider empire. Little understanding the sources
of her own greatness, Athens would go to war: peace is
the interest of a seat of commerce and the arts; but

to war she went; yet to her, whether peace or war, it mattered not. The political power of Athens waned and disappeared; kingdoms rose and fell; centuries rolled away,—they did but bring fresh triumphs to the city of the poet and the sage. There at length the swarthy Moor and Spaniard were seen to meet the blue-eyed Gaul; and the Cappadocian, late subject of Mithridates, gazed without alarm at the haughty conquering Roman. Revolution after revolution passed over the face of Europe, as well as of Greece, but still she was there,— Athens, the city of mind,—as radiant, as splendid, as delicate, as young, as ever she had been. (*H. S.* III. 19f.)

A CONFINED triangle, perhaps fifty miles its greatest length, and thirty its greatest breadth; two elevated rocky barriers, meeting at an angle; three prominent mountains, commanding the plain—Parnes, Pentelicus, and Hymettus; an unsatisfactory soil; some streams, not always full;— such is about the report which the agent of a London company would have made of Attica. He would report that the climate was mild; the hills were limestone; there was plenty of good marble; more pasture-land than at first survey might have been expected, sufficient certainly for sheep and goats; fisheries productive; silver mines once, but long since worked out; figs fair; oil first-rate; olives in profusion.

But what he would not think of noting down was, that that olive-tree was so choice in nature and so noble in shape, that it excited a religious veneration; and that it took so kindly to the light soil as to expand into woods upon the open plain, and to climb up and fringe the hills. He would not think of writing word to his employers, how that clear air, of which I have spoken, brought out, yet blended and subdued, the colours on the marble, till they had a softness and harmony, for all their richness, which in a picture looks exaggerated, yet is after all within the truth. He would not tell how that same delicate and brilliant atmosphere freshened up the pale olive, till the olive forgot its monotony, and its cheek glowed like the arbutus or beech of the Umbrian hills. He would say nothing of the thyme and thousand fragrant herbs which carpeted Hymettus; he would hear nothing of the hum of its bees; nor take much account of the rare flavour of its honey, since Gozo and Minorca were sufficient for the English demand.

He would look over the Ægean from the height he had ascended; he would follow with his eye the chain of islands, which, starting from the Sunian headland, seemed to offer the fabled divinities of Attica, when they would visit their Ionian cousins, a sort of viaduct thereto across the sea: but this thought would not occur to him, nor any admiration of the dark violet billows with their white edges down below; nor of those graceful, fan-like jets of silver upon the rocks, which slowly rise aloft like water spirits from the deep, then shiver, and break, and spread, and shroud themselves, and disappear, in a soft mist of foam; nor of the gentle, incessant heaving and panting of the whole liquid plain; nor of the long waves, keeping steady time, like a line of soldiery, as they resound upon the hollow shore,—he would not deign to notice that restless living element at all, except to bless his stars that he was not upon it. Nor the distinct detail, nor the refined colouring, nor the graceful outline and roseate golden hue of the jutting crags, nor the bold shadows cast from Otus or Laurium by the declining sun;—our agent of a mercantile firm would not value these matters even at a low figure. Rather we must turn for the sympathy we

seek to yon pilgrim student come from a semi-barbarous
land to that small corner of the earth, as to a shrine,
where he might take his fill of gazing on those emblems
and coruscations of invisible unoriginate perfection. It
was the stranger from a remote province, from Britain
or from Mauritania, who in a scene so different from that
of his chilly, woody swamps, or of his fiery choking sands,
learned at once what a real University must be, by
coming to understand the sort of country, which was
its suitable home. (*H. S.* III 20ff.)

THE ATHENIANS exercised Influence by discarding Law.
It was their boast that they had found out the art of
living well and happily, without working for it. They
professed to do right, not from servile feeling, not because they were obliged, not from fear of command, not
from belief of the unseen, but because it was their nature, because it was so truly pleasant, because it was
such a luxury to do it. Their political bond was good
will and generous sentiment. They were loyal citizens, active, hardy, brave, munificent, from their very love of
what was high, and because the virtuous was the enjoyable, and the enjoyable was the virtuous. They regulated themselves by music, and so danced through life.

Thus, according to Pericles, while, in private and personal matters, each Athenian was suffered to please himself, without any tyrannous public opinion to make
him feel uncomfortable, the same freedom of will did
but unite the people, one and all, in concerns of national interest, because obedience to the magistrates and
the laws was with them a sort of passion, to shrink from
dishonour an instinct, and to repress injustice an indulgence. They could be splendid in their feasts and spectacles without extravagance, because the crowds whom

they attracted from abroad repaid them for the outlay; and such large hospitality did but cherish in them a frank, unsuspicious, and courageous spirit, which better protected them than a pile of state secrets and exclusive laws. Nor did this joyous mode of life relax them, as it might relax a less noble race, for they were warlike without effort, and expert without training, and rich in resource by the gift of nature, and, after their fill of pleasure, they were only more gallant in the field, and more patient and enduring on the march. They cultivated the fine arts with too much taste to be expensive, and they studied the sciences with too much point to become effeminate; debate did not blunt their energy, nor foresight of danger chill their daring; but, as their tragic poet expresses it, "the loves were the attendants upon wisdom, and had a share in the acts of every virtue." Such was the Athenian according to his own account of himself. (*H. S.* iii. 83f.)

ATHENS was of far too fine and dainty a nature for the wear and tear of life;—she needed to be "of sterner stuff," if she was to aspire to the charge of the young and inexperienced. Not all the zeal of the teacher and devotion of the pupil, the thirst of giving and receiving, the exuberance of demand and supply, will avail for a University, unless some provision is made for the maintenance of authority and of discipline, unless the terrors of the Law are added to the persuasives of the Beautiful. Influence was not enough without command. (*H. S.* iii. 85)

MIRACLES, though they contravene the physical laws of the universe, tend to the due fulfilment of its moral laws. (*O. U. S.* p. 196)

ANCIENT Rome had the talent of organization; and she formed a political framework to unite to herself and to each other the countries which she successively conquered. She sent out her legions all over the earth to secure and to govern it. She created establishments which were fitted to last for ever; she brought together a hundred nations into one, and she moulded Europe on a model, which it retains even now;—and this not by a sentiment or an imagination, but by wisdom of policy, and the iron hand of Law. Establishment is the very idea, which the name of Imperial Rome suggests. Athens, on the other hand, was as fertile, indeed, in schools, as Rome in military successes and political institutions; she was as metropolitan a city, and as frequented a capital, as Rome; she drew the world to her, she sent her literature into the world; but still men came and went, in and out, without constraint; and her preachers went to and fro, as they pleased; she sent out her missions by reason of her energy of intellect, and men came on pilgrimage to her from their love for philosophy. (*H. S.* III. 87)

EDUCATION had gone through a course of difficulties, and had a place in the prosperous result. First, carried forth upon the wings of genius, and disseminated by the energy of individual minds, or by the colonizing missions of single cities, Knowledge was irregularly extended to and fro over the spacious regions, of which the Mediterranean is the common basin. Introduced, in course of time, to a more intimate alliance with political power, it received the means, at the date of Alexander and his successors, both of its cultivation and its propagation. It was formally recognized and endowed under the

Ptolemies, and at length became a direct object of the solicitude of the government under the Cæsars. It was honoured and dispensed in every considerable city of the Empire; it tempered the political administration of the conquering people; it civilized the manners of a hundred barbarian conquests; it gradually reconciled uncongenial, and associated distant countries, with each other; while it had ever ministered to the fine arts, it now proceeded to subserve the useful.

It took in hand the reformation of the world's religion; it began to harmonize the legends of discordant worships; it purified the mythology by making it symbolical; it interpreted it, and gave it a moral, and explained away its idolatry. It began to develop a system of ethics, it framed a code of laws: what might not be expected of it, as time went on, were it not for that illiberal, unintelligible, fanatical, abominable sect of Galileans? If they were allowed to make play, and get power, what might not happen? There again Christians were in the way, as hateful to the philosopher, as to the statesman.

Yet in truth it was not in this quarter that the peril of civilization lay: it lay in a very different direction, over against the Empire to the North and North-East, in a black cloud of inexhaustible barbarian populations: and when the storm mounted overhead and broke upon the earth, it was those scorned and detested Galileans, and none but they, the men-haters and God-despisers, who, returning good for evil, housed and lodged the scattered remnants of that old world's wisdom, which had so persecuted them, went forth valiantly to meet the savage destroyer, tamed him without arms, and became the founders of a new and higher civilization. Not a man in Europe now, who talks bravely against the

Church, but owes it to the Church, that he can talk at all. (*H. S.* III. 108f.)

BUT WHAT was to be the process, what the method, what the instruments, what the place, for sheltering the treasures of ancient intellect during the convulsion, of bridging over the abyss, and of linking the old world to the new? In spite of the consolidation of its power, Rome was to go, as all things human go, and vanish for ever. All the fury of the elements was directed against it; and, as a continual dropping wears away the stone, so blow after blow, and revolution after revolution, sufficed at last to heave up, and hurl down, and smash into fragments, the noblest earthly power that ever was. First came the Goth, then the Hun, and then the Lombard. The Goth took possession, but he was of noble nature, and soon lost his barbarism. The Hun came next; he was irreclaimable, but did not stay. The Lombard kept both his savageness and his ground; he appropriated to himself the territory, not the civilization of Italy, fierce as the Hun, and powerful as the Goth, the most tremendous scourge of Heaven. In his dark presence the poor remains of Greek and Roman splendour died away, and the world went rapidly to ruin, material and moral. Alas! the change between Rome in the hey-day of her pride, and in the agony of her judgment! (*H. S.* III. 109f.)

IN THE interval between the barbarian invasions, there was a direct tendency to a revival of what had been trodden down, and a restoration of what had been defaced. The fierce soldier was vanquished by the captive of his sword and bow. The beauty of the southern climate, the richness of its productions, the material splendour of its cities, the majesty of the imperial organization, the spontaneous precision of a routine administration, the influence of religion upon the imagination and the affections, antiquity, rule, name, prescription, and territory, presented to him in visible and recognized forms,—in a word, the conservative power proper to establishments,—awed, overcame, and won, the sensitive and noble savage. "Order is heaven's first law," and bears upon it the impress of divinity; and it has an especial power over those minds which have had least experience of it. The Goth not only took pay, and sought refuge, from the Empire, but, still more, when, instead of dependent, he was lord and master, he found himself absorbed into and assimilated with the civilization, upon which he had violently thrust himself. Had he been left in possession, great revolutions certainly, but not dissolution, would have been the destiny of the social framework; and the tradition of science and of the arts of life would have been unbroken. (*H. S.* III. 116f.)

IT WAS indeed an old, decayed and moribund world, into which Christianity had been cast. The social fabric was overgrown with the corruptions of a thousand years, and was held together, not so much by any common principle, as by the strength of possession and the tenacity of custom. It was too large for public spirit and too artificial for patriotism, and its many religions did but foster in the popular mind division and scepticism. Want of mutual confidence would lead to despondency, inactivity and selfishness. Society was in the slow fever of consumption, which made it restless in proportion as it was feeble. It was powerful, however, to seduce and deprave; nor was there any *locus standi* from which to combat its evils; and the only way of getting on with it was to abandon principle and duty, to take things as they came, and to do as the world did. Worse than all, this encompassing, entangling system of things, was, at the time we speak of, the seat and instrument of a paganism, and then of heresies, not simply contrary, but bitterly hostile, to the Christian profession. Serious men not only had a call, but every inducement which love of life and freedom could supply, to escape from its presence and its sway. (*H. S.* II. 374)

THE MONKS were not dreamy sentimentalists, to fall in love with melancholy winds and purling rills, and waterfalls and nodding groves; but their poetry was the poetry of hard work and hard fare, unselfish hearts and charitable hands. They could plough and reap, they could hedge and ditch, they could drain; they could lop, they could carpenter; they could thatch, they could make hurdles for their huts; they could make a road, they could divert or secure the streamlet's bed, they could bridge a torrent. If their grounds are picturesque, if their views are rich, they made them so, and had, we presume, a right to enjoy the work of their own hands. They found a swamp, a moor, a thicket, a rock, and they made an Eden in the wilderness. They destroyed snakes; they extirpated wild cats, wolves, boars, bears; they put to flight or they converted rovers, outlaws, robbers. The gloom of the forest departed, and the sun, for the first time since the Deluge, shone upon the moist ground. (*H. S.* II. 398)

WHEN [the monks] had in the course of many years gained their peaceful victories, perhaps some new invader came, and with fire and sword undid their slow and persevering toil in an hour. The Hun succeeded to the Goth, the Lombard to the Hun, the Tartar to the Lombard; the Saxon was reclaimed only that the Dane might take his place. Down in the dust lay the labour and civilization of centuries—churches, colleges, cloisters, libraries—and nothing was left to them but to begin all over again; but this they did without grudging, so promptly, cheerfully, and tranquilly, as if it were by some law of nature that the restoration came, and they were like the flowers and shrubs and fruit trees which they reared, and which, when ill-treated, do not take vengeance, or remember evil, but give forth fresh branches, leaves, or blossoms, perhaps in greater profusion, and with richer quality, for the very reason that the old were rudely broken off. If one holy place was desecrated, the monks pitched upon another, and by this time there were rich or powerful men who remembered and loved the past enough to wish to have it restored in the future. (*H. S.* II. 410f.)

TO THE monk heaven was next door; he formed no plans, he had no cares; the ravens of his father Benedict were ever at his side. He "went forth" in his youth "to his work and to his labour" until the evening of life; if he lived a day longer, he did a day's work more; whether he lived many days or few, he laboured on to the end of them. He had no wish to see further in advance of his journey than where he was to make his next stage. He ploughed and sowed, he prayed, he meditated, he studied, he wrote, he taught, and then he died and went to heaven. He made his way into the labyrinthine forest, and he cleared just so much of space as his dwelling required, suffering the high solemn trees and the deep pathless thicket to close him in.

When he began to build, his architecture was suggested by the scene—not the scientific and masterly conception of a great whole with many parts, as the Gothic style in a later age, but plain and inartificial, the adaptation of received fashions to his own purpose, and an addition of chapel to chapel and a wayward growth of cloister, according to the occasion, with half-concealed shrines and unexpected recesses, with paintings on the wall as by a second thought, with an absence of display and a wild, irregular beauty, like that of the woods by which he was at first surrounded.

When he would employ his mind, he turned to Scripture, the Book of books, and there he found a special response to the peculiarities of his vocation; for there supernatural truths stand forth as the trees and flowers of Eden, in a divine disorder, as some awful intricate garden or paradise, which he enjoyed the more because he could not catalogue its wonders. Next he read the Holy Fathers, and there again he recognised a like ungrudging profusion and careless wealth of precept and of consolation.

When he began to compose, still he did so after that mode which nature and revelation had taught him, avoiding curious knowledge, content with incidental ignorance, passing from subject to subject with little regard to system, or care to penetrate beyond his own homestead of thought—and writing, not with the sharp logic of disputants, or the subtle analysis of philosophers, but with the one aim of reflecting in his pages, as in a faithful mirror, the words and works of the Almighty, as they confronted him, whether in Scripture and the Fathers, or in that "mighty maze" of deeds and events, which men call the world's history, but which to him was a Providential Dispensation. (*H. S.* II. 426ff.)

AS THE Apostles went through labours untold, by sea and land, in their charity to souls; so, if robbers, shipwrecks, bad lodging, and scanty fare are trials of zeal, such trials were encountered without hesitation by the martyrs and confessors of science. And as Evangelists had grounded their teaching upon the longing for happiness natural to man, so did these securely rest their cause on the natural thirst for knowledge: and again as the preachers of Gospel peace had often to bewail the ruin which persecution or dissension had brought upon their flourishing colonies, so also did the professors of science often find or flee the ravages of sword or pestilence in those places, which they themselves perhaps in former times had made the seats of religious, honourable, and useful learning. (*H. S.* III. 166)

THE great University of Paris engrossed as its territory the whole south bank of the Seine, and occupied one half, and that the pleasanter half, of the city. King Louis had the island pretty well as his own—it was scarcely more than a fortification; and the north of the river was given over to the nobles and citizens to do what they could with its marshes; but the eligible south, rising from the stream, which swept around its base, to the fair summit of St. Genevieve, with its broad meadows, its vineyards and its gardens, and with the sacred elevation of Montmartre confronting it, all this was the inheritance of the University. There was that pleasant

Pratum, stretching along the river's bank, in which the
students for centuries took their recreation, which Alcuin
seems to mention in his farewell verses to Paris, and
which has given a name to the great Abbey of St. Ger-
main-des-Prés. For long years it was devoted to the
purposes of innocent and healthy enjoyment; but evil
times came on the University; disorder arose within its
precincts, and the fair meadow became the scene of party
brawls; heresy stalked through Europe, and, Germany
and England no longer sending their contingent of students, a heavy debt was the consequence to the academi-
cal body. To let their lands was the only resource left
to them: buildings rose upon it, and spread along the
green sod, and the country at length became town. Great
was the grief and indignation of the doctors and masters
when this catastrophe occurred. "A wretched sight," said
the Proctor of the German nation, "a wretched sight, to
witness the sale of that ancient manor, whither the muses
were wont to wander for retirement and pleasure. Whither
shall the youthful student now betake himself, what relief will he find for his eyes, wearied with intense reading, now that the pleasant stream is taken from him?"
Two centuries and more have passed since this complaint
was uttered, and time has shown that the outward calamity, which it recorded, was but the emblem of the
great moral revolution, which was to follow; till the institution itself has followed its green meadows, into the
region of things which once were and now are not.
(*H. S.* III. 25f.)

ALAS! for centuries past Oxford has lost its prime
honour and boast, as a servant and soldier of the Truth.
Once named the second school of the Church, second only
to Paris, the foster-mother of St. Edward, St. Richard,

St. Thomas Cantilupe, the theatre of great intellects, of
Scotus, the subtle Doctor, of Hales the irrefragable, of
Occam the special, of Bacon the admirable, of Middle-
ton the solid, and of Bradwardine the profound, Oxford
has now lapsed to that level of mere human loveliness
which, in its highest perfection, we admire in Athens.
Nor would it occur to me to speak its name, except that,
even in its sorrowful deprivation, it retains just so much
of that outward lustre which, like the brightness on
the prophet's face, ought to be a ray from an illumination within, as to afford me an illustration of the point
on which I am engaged, viz., what should be the material
dwelling-place and appearance, the local circumstances,
and the secular concomitants of a great University. The
spell which this once loyal daughter of the Church still
exercises upon the foreign visitor, even now when her
true glory is departed, suggests to us how far more majestic, and more touching, how brimful of indescribable
influence would be the presence of a University which
was planted within, not without, Jerusalem—an influence
potent as her truth is strong, wide as her way is world-
wide, and growing, not lessening, by the extent of space
over which its attraction would be exerted. (*H. S.* III. 28)

THERE are those who, having felt the influence of this
ancient school [Oxford], and being smit with its splendour and its sweetness, ask wistfully if never again it
is to be Catholic, or whether at least some footing for
Catholicity may not be found there? All honour and
merit to the charitable and zealous hearts who so inquire! Nor can we dare to tell what in time to come
may be the inscrutable purposes of that grace which is
ever more comprehensive than human hope and aspira-

tion. But for me, from the day I left its walls, I never, for good or bad, have had anticipation of its future; and never for a moment have I had a wish to see again a place which I have never ceased to love, and where I lived for nearly thirty years. (*H. S.* III. 31)

[THE convert Charles Reding, about to leave Oxford,] passed through Bagley wood, and the spires and towers of the University came on his view, hallowed by how many tender associations, lost to him for two whole years, suddenly recovered—recovered to be lost for ever! There lay old Oxford before him, with its hills as gentle and its meadows as green as ever. At the first view of that beloved place he stood still with folded arms, unable to proceed. Each college, each church, he counted them by their pinnacles and turrets. The silver Isis, the grey willows, the far-stretching plains, the dark groves, the distant range of Shotover, the pleasant village where he had lived with Carlton and Sheffield—wood, water, stone, all so calm, so bright, they might have been his, but his they were not. Whatever he was to gain by becoming a Catholic, this he had lost; whatever he was to gain higher and better, at least this and such as this he never could have again. He could not have another Oxford, he could not have the friends of his boyhood and youth in the choice of his manhood.* (*L. G.*, p. 353f.)

THAT training of the intellect, which is best for the individual himself, best enables him to discharge his duties to society. The Philosopher, indeed, and the man of the

* These were Newman's own thoughts when, on becoming a Catholic, he looked upon Oxford, his Alma Mater, for the last time.

world differ in their very notion, but the methods, by which they are respectively formed, are pretty much the same. The Philosopher has the same command of matters of thought, which the true citizen and gentleman has of matters of business and conduct. If then a practical end must be assigned to a University course, I say it is that of training good members of society. Its art is the art of social life, and its end is fitness for the world.

It neither confines its views to particular professions on the one hand, nor creates heroes or inspires genius on the other. Works indeed of genius fall under no art; heroic minds come under no rule; a University is not a birthplace of poets or of immortal authors, of founders of schools, leaders of colonies, or conquerors of nations. It does not promise a generation of Aristotles or Newtons, of Napoleons or Washingtons, of Raphaels or Shakespeares, though such miracles of nature it has before now contained within its precincts. Nor is it content on the other hand with forming the critic or the experimentalist, the economist or the engineer, though such too it includes within its scope. But a University training is the great ordinary means to a great but ordinary end; it aims at raising the intellectual tone of society, at cultivating the public mind, at purifying the national taste, at supplying true principles to popular enthusiasm and fixed aims to popular aspiration, at giving enlargement and sobriety to the ideas of the age, at facilitating the exercise of political power, and refining the intercourse of private life.

It is the education which gives a man a clear conscious view of his own opinions and judgments, a truth in developing them, an eloquence in expressing them, and a force in urging them. It teaches him to see things as they are, to go right to the point, to disentangle a skein of thought, to detect what is sophistical, and to discard what is irrelevant. It prepares him to fill any post with credit, and to master any subject with facility. It shows him how to accommodate himself to others, how to throw himself into their state of mind, how to bring before them his own, how to influence them, how to come to an understanding with them, how to bear with them.

He is at home in any society, he has common ground with every class; he knows when to speak and when to be silent; he is able to converse, he is able to listen; he can ask a question pertinently, and gain a lesson seasonably, when he has nothing to impart himself; he is ever ready, yet never in the way; he is a pleasant companion, and a comrade you can depend upon; he knows when to be serious and when to trifle, and he has a sure tact which enables him to trifle with gracefulness and to be serious with effect. He has the repose of a mind which lives in itself, while it lives in the world, and which has resources for its happiness at home when it cannot go abroad. He has a gift which serves him in public, and supports him in retirement, without which good fortune is but vulgar, and with which failure and disappointment have a charm. The art which tends to make a man all this, is in the object which it pursues as useful as the art of wealth or the art of health, though it is less susceptible of method, and less tangible, less certain, less complete in its result. (*I. of U.*, p. 177f.)

rr is almost a definition of a gentleman to say he is one who never inflicts pain. This description is both refined and, as far as it goes, accurate. The true gentleman in like manner carefully avoids whatever may cause a jar or a jolt in the minds of those with whom he is cast;—all clashing of opinion, or collision of feeling, all restraint, or suspicion, or gloom, or resentment; his great concern being to make every one at their ease and at home. He has his eyes on all his company; he is tender towards the bashful, gentle towards the distant, and merciful towards the absurd; he can recollect to whom he is speaking; he guards against unseasonable allusions, or topics which may irritate; he is seldom prominent in conversation, and never wearisome. He makes light of favours while he does them, and seems to be receiving when he is conferring. He never speaks of himself except when compelled, never defends himself by a mere retort, he has no ears for slander or gossip, is scrupulous in imputing motives to those who interfere with him, and interprets everything for the best. He is never mean or little in his disputes, never takes unfair advantage, never mistakes personalities or sharp sayings for arguments, or insinuates evil which he dare not say out.

He has too much good sense to be affronted at insults, he is too well employed to remember injuries, and too indolent to bear malice. He is patient, forbearing, and resigned, on philosophical principles; he submits to pain, because it is inevitable, to bereavement, because it is irreparable, and to death, because it is his destiny. If he engages in controversy of any kind, his disciplined intellect preserves him from the blundering discourtesy of better, perhaps, but less educated minds; who, like blunt weapons, tear and hack instead of cutting clean, who mistake the point in argument, waste their strength on trifles, misconceive their adversary, and leave the question more involved than they find it. He may be right or wrong in his opinion, but he is too clear-headed to be unjust; he is as simple as he is forcible, and as brief as he is decisive. Nowhere shall we find greater candour, consideration, indulgence: he throws himself into the minds of his opponents, he accounts for their mistakes. He knows the weakness of human reason as well as its strength, its province and its limits.

If he be an unbeliever, he will be too profound and large-minded to ridicule religion or to act against it; he is too wise to be a dogmatist or fanatic in his infidelity. He respects piety and devotion; he even supports institutions as venerable, beautiful, or useful, to which he does not assent; he honours the ministers of religion, and it contents him to decline its mysteries without assailing or denouncing them. He is a friend of religious toleration, and that, not only because his philosophy has taught him to look on all forms of faith with an impartial eye, but also from the gentleness and effeminacy of feeling, which is the attendant on civilization.

Not that he may not hold a religion too, in his own way, even when he is not a Christian. In that case his religion is one of imagination and sentiment; it is the embodiment of those ideas of the sublime, majestic, and beautiful, without which there can be no large philosophy. Sometimes he acknowledges the being of God, sometimes he invests an unknown principle or quality with the attributes of perfection. And this deduction of his reason, or creation of his fancy, he makes the occasion of such excellent thoughts, and the starting-point of so varied and systematic a teaching, that he even seems like a disciple of Christianity itself. (*I of U.*, p. 208ff.)

IN DEFAULT of a recognized term, I have called the perfection or virtue of the intellect by the name of philosophy, philosophical knowledge, enlargement of mind, or illumination; terms which are not uncommonly given to

it by writers of this day: but, whatever name we bestow
on it, it is, I believe, as a matter of history, the business
of a University to make this intellectual culture its direct
scope, or to employ itself in the education of the intellect,
—just as the work of a Hospital lies in healing the sick
or wounded, of a Riding or Fencing School, or of a
Gymnasium, in exercising the limbs, of an Almshouse, in
aiding and solacing the old, of an Orphanage, in pro-
tecting innocence, of a Penitentiary, in restoring the
guilty. I say, a University, taken in its bare idea, and
before we view it as an instrument of the Church, has
this object and this mission; it contemplates neither
moral impression nor mechanical production; it professes
to exercise the mind neither in art nor in duty; its function is intellectual culture; here it may leave its scholars,
and it has done its work when it has done as much as
this. It educates the intellect to reason well in all matters,
to reach out towards truth, and to grasp it.

In my foregoing Discourse I illustrated this in various
ways. I said that the intellect must have an excellence
of its own, for there was nothing which had not its specific good; that the word "educate" would not be used
of intellectual culture, as it is used, had not the intellect
had an end of its own; that, had it not such an end, there
would be no meaning in calling certain intellectual exercises "liberal," in contrast with "useful," as is commonly done; that the very notion of a philosophical
temper implied it, for it threw us back upon research
and system as ends in themselves, distinct from effects
and works of any kind; that a philosophical scheme of
knowledge, or system of sciences, could not, from the
nature of the case, issue in any one definite art or pursuit, as its end; and that, on the other hand, the discovery and contemplation of truth, to which research and

systematizing led, were surely sufficient ends, though
nothing beyond them were added, and that they had ever
been accounted sufficient by mankind. (*I. of U.*, p. 125f.)

I SUPPOSE the *prima-facie* view which the public at
large would take of a University, considering it as a
place of Education, is nothing more or less than a place
for acquiring a great deal of knowledge on a great many
subjects. Memory is one of the first developed of the
mental faculties; a boy's business when he goes to school
is to learn, that is, to store up things in his memory.
For some years his intellect is little more than an instrument for taking in facts, or a receptacle for storing them;
he welcomes them as fast as they come to him; he lives
on what is without; he has his eyes ever about him; he
has a lively susceptibility of impressions; he imbibes
information of every kind; and little does he make his
own in a true sense of the word, living rather upon his
neighbours all around him.

He has opinions, religious, political and literary, and,
for a boy, is very positive in them and sure about them;
but he gets them from his schoolfellows, or his masters,
or his parents, as the case may be. Such as he is in his
other relations, such also is he in his school exercises;
his mind is observant, sharp, ready, retentive; he is
almost passive in the acquisition of knowledge. I say
this in no disparagement of the idea of a clever boy.
Geography, chronology, history, language, natural history, he heaps up the matter of these studies as treasures
for a future day. It is the seven years of plenty with
him: he gathers in by handfuls, like the Egyptians, without counting; and though, as time goes on, there is exercise for his argumentative powers in the Elements of

Mathematics, and for his taste in the Poets and Orators, still, while at school, or at least, till quite the last years of his time, he acquires, and little more; and when he is leaving for the University, he is mainly the creature of foreign influences and circumstances, and made up of accidents, homogeneous or not, as the case may be.

Moreover, the moral habits, which are a boy's praise, encourage and assist this result; that is, diligence, assiduity, regularity, despatch, persevering application; for these are the direct conditions of acquisition, and naturally lead to it. Acquirements, again, are emphatically producible, and at a moment; they are a something to show, both for master and scholar; an audience, even though ignorant themselves of the subject of an examination, can comprehend when questions are answered and when they are not. Here again is a reason why mental culture is in the minds of men identified with the acquisition of knowledge.

The same notion possesses the public mind, when it passes on from the thought of a school to that of a University: and with the best of reasons so far as this, that there is no true culture without acquirements, and that philosophy presupposes knowledge. It requires a great deal of reading, or a wide range of information, to warrant us in putting forth our opinions on any serious subject; and without such learning the most original mind may be able indeed to dazzle, to amuse, to refute, to perplex, but not to come to any useful result or any trustworthy conclusion.

There are indeed persons who profess a different view of the matter, and even act upon it. Every now and then you will find a person of vigorous or fertile mind, who relies upon his own resources, despises all former authors, and gives the world, with the utmost fearlessness,

his views upon religion, or history, or any other popular
subject. And his works may sell for a while; he may get
a name in his day; but this will be all. His readers are
sure to find on the long run that his doctrines are mere
theories, and not the expression of facts, that they are
chaff instead of bread, and then his popularity drops as
suddenly as it rose.

Knowledge then is the indispensable condition of expansion of mind, and the instrument of attaining to it;
this cannot be denied, it is ever to be insisted on; I begin
with it as a first principle; however, the very truth of it
carries men too far, and confirms to them the notion that
it is the whole of the matter. A narrow mind is thought
to be that which contains little knowledge; and an en-
larged mind, that which holds a great deal; and what
seems to put the matter beyond dispute is, the fact of
the great number of studies which are pursued in a University, by its very profession.

Lectures are given on every kind of subject; examinations are held; prizes awarded. There are moral, meta-
physical, physical Professors; Professors of languages, of
history, of mathematics, of experimental science. Lists of
questions are published, wonderful for their range and
depth, variety and difficulty; treatises are written, which
carry upon their very face the evidence of extensive reading or multifarious information; what then is wanting
for mental culture to a person of large reading and
scientific attainments? what is grasp of mind but acquirement? where shall philosophical repose be found,
but in the consciousness and enjoyment of large intellectual possessions?

And yet this notion is, I conceive, a mistake: the end
of a Liberal Education is not mere knowledge. (*I. of U.*,
p. 127ff.)

[FALSE intellectual enlargement is experienced] the first time the mind comes across the arguments and speculations of unbelievers, and feels what a novel light they cast upon what he has hitherto accounted sacred; and still more, if it gives in to them and embraces them, and throws off as so much prejudice what it has hitherto held, and, as if waking from a dream, begins to realize to its imagination that there is now no such thing as law and the transgression of law, that sin is a phantom, and punishment a bugbear, that it is free to sin, free to enjoy the world and the flesh; and still further, when it does enjoy them, and reflects that it may think and hold just what it will, that "the world is all before it where to choose," and what system to build up as its own private persuasion; when this torrent of wilful thoughts rushes over and inundates it, who will deny that the fruit of the tree of knowledge, or what the mind takes for knowledge, has made it one of the gods, with a sense of expansion and elevation,—an intoxication in reality, still, so far as the subjective state of the mind goes, an illumination? Hence the fanaticism of individuals or nations, who suddenly cast off their Maker. Their eyes are opened; and, like the judgment-stricken king in the Tragedy, they see two suns, and a magic universe, out of which they look back upon their former state of faith and innocence with a sort of contempt and indignation, as if they were then but fools, and the dupes of imposture.

On the other hand, Religion has its own enlargement, and an enlargement, not of tumult, but of peace. It is often remarked of uneducated persons, who have hitherto thought little of the unseen world, that, on their turning to God, looking into themselves, regulating their hearts, reforming their conduct, and meditating on death and judgment, heaven and hell, they seem to become, in point of intellect, different beings from what they were. Before, they took things as they came, and thought no more of one thing than another. But now every event has a meaning; they have their own estimate of whatever happens to them; they are mindful of times and seasons, and compare the present with the past; and the world, no longer dull, monotonous, unprofitable, and hopeless, is a various and complicated drama, with parts and an object, and an awful moral. (*I. of U.*, p. 132f.)

[TRUE intellectual] enlargement consists, not merely in the passive reception into the mind of a number of ideas hitherto unknown to it, but in the mind's energetic and simultaneous action upon and towards and among those new ideas, which are rushing in upon it. It is the action of a formative power, reducing to order and meaning the matter of our acquirements; it is a making the objects of our knowledge subjectively our own, or, to use a familiar word, it is a digestion of what we receive, into the substance of our previous state of thought; and without this no enlargement is said to follow. There is no enlargement, unless there be a comparison of ideas one with another, as they come before the mind, and a systematizing of them. We feel our minds to be growing and expanding *then*, when we not only learn, but refer what we learn to what we know already.

It is not the mere addition to our knowledge that is the illumination; but the locomotion, the movement onwards, of that mental centre, to which both what we know, and what we are learning, the accumulating mass of our acquirements, gravitates. And therefore a truly great intellect, and recognized to be such by the common opinion of mankind, such as the intellect of Aristotle, or of St. Thomas, or of Newton, or of Goethe (I purposely take instances within and without the Catholic pale, when I would speak of the intellect as such), is one which takes a connected view of old and new, past and present, far and near, and which has an insight into the influence of all these one on another; without which there is no whole, and no centre. It possesses the knowledge, not only of things, but also of their mutual and true relations; knowledge, not merely considered as acquirement but as philosophy.

Accordingly, when this analytical, distributive, harmonizing process is away, the mind experiences no enlargement, and is not reckoned as enlightened or comprehensive, whatever it may add to its knowledge. For instance, a great memory, as I have already said, does not make a philosopher, any more than a dictionary can be called a grammar. There are men who embrace in their minds a vast multitude of ideas, but with little sensibility about their real relations towards each other. These may be antiquarians, annalists, naturalists; they may be learned in the law; they may be versed in statistics; they are most useful in their own place; I should shrink from speaking disrespectfully of them; still, there is nothing in such attainments to guarantee the absence of narrowness of mind. If they are nothing more than well-read men, or men of information, they have not what specially deserves the name of culture of mind, or fulfils the type of Liberal Education. (*I. of U.*, p. 134f.)

WE SOMETIMES fall in with persons who have seen much of the world, and of the men who, in their day, have played a conspicuous part in it, but who generalize nothing, and have no observation, in the true sense of the word. They abound in information in detail, curious and entertaining, about men and things; and, having lived under the influence of no very clear or settled principles, religious or political, they speak of every one and every thing, only as so many phenomena, which are complete in themselves, and lead to nothing, not discussing them, or teaching any truth, or instructing the hearer, but simply talking. No one would say that these persons, well informed as they are, had attained to any great culture of intellect or to philosophy.

The case is the same still more strikingly where the persons in question are beyond dispute men of inferior powers and deficient education. Perhaps they have been much in foreign countries, and they receive, in a passive, otiose, unfruitful way, the various facts which are forced upon them there. Seafaring men, for example, range from one end of the earth to the other; but the multiplicity of eternal objects, which they have encountered, forms no symmetrical and consistent picture upon their imagination; they see the tapestry of human life, as it were on the wrong side, and it tells no story. They sleep, and they rise up, and they find themselves, now in Europe, now in Asia; they see visions of great cities and wild regions; they are in the marts of commerce, or amid the islands of the South; they gaze on Pompey's Pillar, or on the Andes; and nothing which meets them carries them forward or backward, to any idea beyond itself. Nothing has a drift or relation; nothing has a history or a promise. Every thing stands by itself, and comes and goes in its turn, like the shifting scenes of a show, which leave the spectator where he was.

Perhaps you are near such a man on a particular occasion, and expect him to be shocked or perplexed at something which occurs; but one thing is much the same to

him as another, or, if he is perplexed, it is as not knowing
what to say, whether it is right to admire, or to ridicule,
or to disapprove, while conscious that some expression of
opinion is expected from him; for in fact he has no standard of judgment at all, and no landmarks to guide him
to a conclusion. Such is mere acquisition, and, I repeat,
no one would dream of calling it philosophy. (*I. of U.*,
p. 135f.)

THAT only is true enlargement of mind which is the
power of viewing many things at once as one whole, of
referring them severally to their true place in the universal system, of understanding their respective values,
and determining their mutual dependence. Thus is that
form of Universal Knowledge, of which I have on a
former occasion spoken, set up in the individual intellect,
and constitutes its perfection. Possessed of this real illumination, the mind never views any part of the extended
subject-matter of Knowledge without recollecting that it
is but a part, or without the associations which spring
from this recollection. It makes everything in some sort
lead to everything else; it would communicate the image
of the whole to every separate portion, till that whole
becomes in imagination like a spirit, everywhere pervading and penetrating its component parts, and giving
them one definite meaning. Just as our bodily organs,
when mentioned, recall their function in the body, as
the word "creation" suggests the Creator, and "subjects"
a sovereign, so in the mind of the Philosopher, as we are
abstractedly conceiving of him, the elements of the physical and moral world, sciences, arts, pursuits, ranks, offices,
events, opinions, individualities, are all viewed as one,
with correlative functions, and as gradually by succes-

sive combinations converging, one and all, to the true centre.

To have even a portion of this illuminative reason and true philosophy is the highest state to which nature can aspire, in the way of intellect; it puts the mind above the influences of chance and necessity, above anxiety, suspense, unsettlement, and superstition, which is the lot of the many. Men, whose minds are possessed with some one object, take exaggerated views of its importance, are feverish in the pursuit of it, make it the measure of things which are utterly foreign to it, and are startled and despond if it happens to fail them. They are ever in alarm or in transport. Those on the other hand who have no object or principle whatever to hold by, lose their way every step they take. They are thrown out, and do not know what to think or say, at every fresh juncture; they have no view of persons, or occurrences, or facts, which come suddenly upon them, and they hang upon the opinion of others for want of internal resources.

But the intellect, which has been disciplined to the perfection of its powers, which knows, and thinks while it knows, which has learned to leaven the dense mass of facts and events with the elastic force of reason, such an intellect cannot be partial, cannot be exclusive, cannot be impetuous, cannot be at a loss, cannot but be patient, collected, and majestically calm, because it discerns the end in every beginning, the origin in every end, the law in every interruption, the limit in each delay; because it ever knows where it stands, and how its path lies from one point to another.

There are men who, when in difficulties, originate at the moment vast ideas or dazzling projects; who, under the influence of excitement, are able to cast a light, almost as if from inspiration, on a subject or course of action which comes before them; who have a sudden presence of mind equal to any emergency, rising with the occasion, and an undaunted magnanimous bearing, and an energy and keenness which is but made intense by opposition. This is genius, this is heroism; it is the exhibition of a natural gift, which no culture can teach, at which no Institution can aim: here, on the contrary, we are concerned, not with mere nature, but with training and teaching.

That perfection of the Intellect, which is the result of Education, and its *beau ideal,* to be imparted to individuals in their respective measures, is the clear, calm, accurate vision and comprehension of all things, as far as the finite mind can embrace them, each in its place, and with its own characteristics upon it. It is almost prophetic from its knowledge of history; it is almost heart-searching from its knowledge of human nature; it has almost supernatural charity from its freedom from littleness and prejudice; it has almost the repose of faith, because nothing can startle it; it has almost the beauty and harmony of heavenly contemplation, so intimate is it with the eternal order of things and the music of the spheres. (*I. of U.,* p. 136ff.)

I WILL tell you what has been the practical error of the last twenty years,—not to load the memory of the student with a mass of undigested knowledge, but to force upon him so much that he has rejected all. It has been the error of distracting and enfeebling the mind by an unmeaning profusion of subjects; of implying that a smattering in a dozen branches of study is not shallowness, which it really is, but enlargement, which it is not;

of considering an acquaintance with the learned names of things and persons, and the possession of clever duo-decimos, and attendance on eloquent lecturers, and membership with scientific institutions, and the sight of the experiments of a platform and the specimens of a museum, that all this was not dissipation of mind, but progress. All things now are to be learned at once, not first one thing, then another, not one well, but many badly. Learning is to be without exertion, without attention, without toil; without grounding, without advance, without finishing. There is to be nothing individual in it; and this, forsooth, is the wonder of the age.

What the steam engine does with matter, the printing-press is to do with mind; it is to act mechanically, and the population is to be passively, almost unconsciously enlightened, by the mere multiplication and dissemination of volumes. Whether it be the school-boy, or the school-girl, or the youth at college, or the mechanic in the town, or the politician in the senate, all have been the victims in one way or other of this most preposterous and pernicious of delusions. Wise men have lifted up their voices in vain; and at length, lest their own institutions should be outshone and should disappear in the folly of the hour, they have been obliged, as far as they could with a good conscience, to humour a spirit which they could not withstand, and make temporizing concessions at which they could not but inwardly smile. (*I. of U.*, p. 142f.)

IF I had to choose between a so-called University, which dispensed with residence and tutorial superintendence, and gave its degrees to any person who passed an examination in a wide range of subjects, and a University which had no professors or examinations at all, but merely brought a number of young men together for three or four years, and then sent them away as the University of Oxford is said to have done some sixty years since, if I were asked which of these two methods was the better discipline of the intellect,—mind, I do not say which is *morally* the better, for it is plain that compulsory study must be a good and idleness an intolerable mischief,—but if I must determine which of the two courses was the more successful in training, moulding, enlarging the mind, which sent out men the more fitted for their secular duties, which produced better public men, men of the world, men whose names would descend to posterity, I have no hesitation in giving the preference to that University which did nothing, over that which exacted of its members an acquaintance with every science under the sun. (*I. of U.*, p. 145)

IT IS a contradiction in terms to attempt a sinless Literature of sinful man. You may gather together something very great and high, something higher than any Literature ever was; and when you have done so, you will find that it is not Literature at all. You will have simply left the delineation of man, as such, and have substituted for it, as far as you have had anything to substitute, that of man, as he is or might be, under certain special advantages. Give up the study of man, as such, if so it must be; but say you do so. Do not say you are studying him, his history, his mind and his heart, when you are studying something else.

Man is a being of genius, passion, intellect, conscience, power. He exercises these various gifts in various ways, in great deeds, in great thoughts, in heroic acts, in hateful crimes. He founds states, he fights battles, he builds cities, he ploughs the forest, he subdues the elements, he rules his kind. He creates vast ideas, and influences many generations. He takes a thousand shapes, and undergoes a thousand fortunes. Literature records them all to the life.

He pours out his fervid soul in poetry; he sways to and fro, he soars, he dives, in his restless speculations; his lips drop eloquence; he touches the canvas, and it glows with beauty; he sweeps the strings, and they thrill with an ecstatic meaning. He looks back into himself, and he reads his own thoughts, and notes them down; he looks out into the universe, and tells over and celebrates the elements and principles of which it is the product. (*I. of U.*, p. 229f.)

NOT till the whole human race is made new will its literature be pure and true. If you would in fact have a literature of saints, first of all have a nation of them. (*I. of U.*, p. 231)

THE structure of the Inspired Word is undeniably *not* the reflection or picture of the many, but of the few; it is no picture of life, but an anticipation of death and judgment. Human literature is about all things, grave or gay, painful or pleasant; but the Inspired Word views them only in one aspect, and as they tend to one scope. It gives us little insight into the fertile developments of mind; it has no terms in its vocabulary to express with exactness the intellect and its separate faculties: it knows nothing of genius, fancy, wit, invention, presence of mind, resource. It does not discourse of empire, commerce, enterprise, learning, philosophy, or the fine arts. Slightly too does it touch on the more simple and innocent courses

of nature and their reward. Little does it say of those
temporal blessings which rest upon our worldly occupations, and make them easy; of the blessings which we
derive from the sunshine day and the serene night, from
the succession of the seasons, and the produce of the
earth. Little about our recreations and our daily domestic
comforts; little about the ordinary occasions of festivity
and mirth, which sweeten human life; and nothing at all
about various pursuits or amusements, which it would be
going too much into detail to mention. We read indeed
of the feast when Isaac was weaned, and of Jacob's court-
ship, and of the religious merry-makings of holy Job;
but exceptions, such as these, do but remind us what
might be in Scripture, and is not. If then by Literature
is meant the manifestation of human nature in human
language, you will seek for it in vain except in the world.
(*I. of U.*, p. 231f.)

WHY do we educate, except to prepare for the world?
Why do we cultivate the intellect of the many beyond
the first elements of knowledge, except for this world?
Will it be much matter in the world to come whether
our bodily health or whether our intellectual strength was
more or less, except of course as this world is in all its
circumstances a trial for the next? If then a University
is a direct preparation for this world, let it be what it
professes. It is not a Convent, it is not a Seminary; it is
a place to fit men of the world for the world. We cannot possibly keep them from plunging into the world,
with all its ways and principles and maxims, when their
time comes; but we can prepare them against what is
inevitable; and it is not the way to learn to swim in
troubled waters, never to have gone into them.

Proscribe (I do not merely say particular authors, particular works, particular passages) but Secular Literature as such; cut out from your class books all broad manifestations of the natural man; and those manifestations are waiting for your pupil's benefit at the very doors of your lecture room in living and breathing substance. They will meet him there in all the charm of novelty, and all the fascination of genius or of amiableness. To-day a pupil, to-morrow a member of the great world: to-day confined to the Lives of the Saints, to-morrow thrown upon Babel;—thrown on Babel, without the honest indulgence of wit and humour and imagination having ever been permitted to him, without any fastidiousness of taste wrought into him, without any rule given him for discriminating "the precious from the vile," beauty from sin, the truth from the sophistry of nature, what is innocent from what is poison.

You have refused him the masters of human thought, who would in some sense have educated him, because of their incidental corruption: you have shut up from him those whose thoughts strike home to our hearts, whose words are proverbs, whose names are indigenous to all the world, who are the standard of their mother tongue, and the pride and boast of their countrymen, Homer, Ariosto, Cervantes, Shakespeare, because the old Adam smelt rank in them; and for what have you reserved him? You have given him "a liberty unto" the multitudinous blasphemy of his day; you have made him free of its newspapers, its reviews, its magazines, its novels, its controversial pamphlets, of its Parliamentary debates, its law proceedings, its platform speeches, its songs, its drama, its theatre, of its enveloping, stifling atmosphere of death. You have succeeded but in this,—in making the world his University.

Difficult as the question may be, and much as it may try the judgments and even divide the opinions of zealous and religious Catholics, I cannot feel any doubt myself that the Church's true policy is not to aim at the exclusion of Literature from Secular Schools, but at her own admission into them. Let her do for Literature in one way what she does for Science in another; each has its imperfection, and she has her remedy for each. She fears no knowledge, but she purifies all; she represses no element of our nature, but cultivates the whole. Science is grave, methodical, logical; with Science then she argues, and opposes reason to reason. Literature does not argue, but declaims and insinuates; it is multiform and versatile: it persuades instead of convincing, it seduces, it carries captive; it appeals to the sense of honour, or to the imagination, or to the stimulus of curiosity; it makes its way by means of gaiety, satire, romance, the beautiful, the pleasurable.

Is it wonderful that with an agent like this the Church should claim to deal with a vigour corresponding to its restlessness, to interfere in its proceedings with a higher hand, and to wield an authority in the choice of its studies and of its books which would be tyrannical, if reason and fact were the only instruments of its conclusions? But anyhow, her principle is one and the same throughout; not to prohibit truth of any kind, but to see that no doctrines pass under the name of Truth but those which claim it rightfully. (*I. of U.*, p. 232ff.)

THERE must ever be something assumed ultimately which is incapable of proof, and without which our conclusion will be as illogical as Faith is apt to seem to men of the world. (*O. U. S.*, p. 213)

THE Philosophy of Utility has at least done its work; and I grant it,—it aimed low, but it has fulfilled its aim. If that man [Bacon] of great intellect who has been its Prophet in the conduct of life played false to his own professions, he was not bound by his philosophy to be true to his friend or faithful in his trust. Moral virtue was not the line in which he undertook to instruct men; and though, as the poet calls him, he were the "meanest" of mankind, he was so in what may be called his private capacity and without any prejudice to the theory of induction. He had a right to be so, if he chose, for any thing that the Idols of the den or the theatre had to say to the contrary. His mission was the increase of physical enjoyment and social comfort; and most wonderfully, most awfully has he fulfilled his conception and his design.

Almost day by day have we fresh and fresh shoots, and buds, and blossoms, which are to ripen into fruit, on that magical tree of Knowledge which he planted, and to which none of us perhaps, except the very poor, but owes, if not his present life, at least his daily food, his health, and general well-being. He was the divinely provided minister of temporal benefits to all of us so great, that, whatever I am forced to think of him as a man, I have not the heart, from mere gratitude, to speak of him severely. And, in spite of the tendencies of his philosophy, which are, as we see at this day, to depreciate, or to trample on Theology, he has himself, in his writings, gone out of his way, as if with a prophetic misgiving of those tendencies, to insist on it as the instrument of that beneficent Father, who, when He came on earth in visible form, took on Him first and most prominently the office of assuaging the bodily wounds of human nature.

Alas, that men, in the action of life or in their heart of hearts, are not what they seem to be in their moments of excitement, or in their trances or intoxications of genius,—so good, so noble, so serene! Alas, that Bacon too in his own way should after all be but the fellow of those heathen philosophers who in their disadvantages had some excuse for their inconsistency, and who surprise us rather in what they did say than in what they did not do! Alas, that he too, like Socrates or Seneca, must be stripped of his holy-day coat, which looks so fair, and should be but a mockery amid his most majestic gravity of phrase; and, for all his vast abilities, should, in the littleness of his own moral being, but typify the intellectual narrowness of his school!

However, granting all this, heroism after all was not his philosophy:—I cannot deny he has abundantly achieved what he proposed. His is simply a Method whereby bodily discomforts and temporal wants are to be most effectually removed from the greatest number; and already, before it has shown any signs of exhaustion, the gifts of nature, in their most artificial shapes and luxurious profusion and diversity, from all quarters of the earth, are, it is undeniable, by its means brought even to our doors, and we rejoice in them. (*I. of U.*, p. 117ff.)

[ONE reason for the prejudice of physical philosophers against theology] is to be found in the difference of method by which truths are gained in theology and in physical science. Induction is the instrument of Physics, and deduction only is the instrument of Theology. Revelation is all in all in doctrine; the Apostles its sole depository, the inferential method its sole instrument, and ecclesiastical authority its sole sanction. The Divine Voice has spoken once for all, and the only question is about its meaning. Now this process, as far as it was reasoning, was the very mode of reasoning which, as regards physical knowledge, the school of Bacon has superseded by the inductive method: no wonder, then, that that school should be irritated and indignant to find that a subject-matter remains still, in which their favourite instrument has no office; no wonder that they rise up against this memorial of an antiquated system, as an eyesore and an insult; and no wonder that the very force and dazzling success of their own method in its own departments should sway or bias unduly the religious sentiments of any persons who come under its influence.

They assert that no new truth can be gained by deduction; Catholics assent, but add, that, as regards religious truth, they have not to seek at all, for they have it already. Christian Truth is purely of revelation; that revelation we can but explain, we cannot increase, except relatively to our own apprehensions; without it we should have known nothing of its contents, with it we know just as much as its contents, and nothing more. And, as it was given by a divine act independent of man, so will it remain in spite of man. Niebuhr may revolutionize history, Lavoisier chemistry, Newton astronomy; but God Himself is the author as well as the subject of Theology. When Truth can change, its Revelation can change; when human reason can outreason the Omniscient, then may it supersede His work.

Avowals such as these fall strange upon the ear of men whose first principle is the search after truth, and whose starting-points of search are things material and sensible. They scorn any process of enquiry not founded on experiment; the Mathematics indeed they endure, because that science deals with ideas, not with facts, and leads to conclusions hypothetical rather than real; "Metaphysics" they even use as a by-word of reproach; and Ethics they admit only on condition that it gives up conscience as its scientific ground, and bases itself on tangible utility: but as to Theology, they cannot deal with it, they cannot master it, and so they simply outlaw it and ignore it. Catholicism, forsooth, "confines the intellect," because it holds that God's intellect is greater than theirs, and that what He has done, man cannot improve. (*I. of U.*, p. 222ff.)

INDEPENDENT of direct instruction on the part of Superiors, there is a sort of self-education in the academic institutions of Protestant England; a characteristic tone of thought, a recognized standard of judgment is found in them, which as developed in the individual who is submitted to it, becomes a twofold source of strength to him, both from the distinct stamp it impresses on his mind, and from the bond of union which it creates between him and others,—effects which are shared by the authorities of the place, for they themselves have been educated in it, and at all times are exposed to the influence of its ethical atmosphere.

Here then is a real teaching, whatever be its standards and principles, true or false; and it at least tends towards cultivation of the intellect; it at least recognizes that knowledge is something more than a sort of passive reception of scraps and details; it is a something, and it does a something, which never will issue from the most strenuous efforts of a set of teachers, with no mutual sympathies and no intercommunion, of a set of examiners with no opinions which they dare profess, and with no common principles, who are teaching or questioning a set of youths who do not know them, and do not know each other, on a large number of subjects, different in kind, and connected by no wide philosophy, three times a week, or three times a year, or once in three years, in chill lecture-rooms or on a pompous anniversary. (*I. of U.*, p. 147f.)

AS IN the human frame there is a living principle, acting upon it and through it by means of volition, so, behind the veil of the visible universe, there is an invisible, intelligent Being, acting on and through it, as and when He will. Further, I mean that this invisible Agent is in no sense a soul of the world, after the analogy of human nature, but, on the contrary, is absolutely distinct from the world, as being its Creator, Upholder, Governor, and Sovereign Lord. Here we are at once brought into the circle of doctrines which the idea of God embodies. I mean then by the Supreme Being, one who is simply self-dependent, and the only Being who is such; moreover, that He is without beginning or Eternal, and the only Eternal; that in consequence He has lived a whole eternity by Himself; and hence that he is all-sufficient, sufficient for His own blessedness, and all-blessed, and ever-blessed.

Further, I mean a Being, who having these prerogatives, has the Supreme Good, or rather is the Supreme Good, or has all the attributes of Good in infinite intenseness; all wisdom, all truth, all justice, all love, all holiness, all beautifulness; who is omnipotent, omniscient, omnipresent; ineffably one, absolutely perfect; and such, that what we do not know and cannot even imagine of Him, is far more wonderful than what we do and can. I mean One who is sovereign over His own will and actions, though always according to the eternal Rule of right and wrong, which is Himself. I mean, moreover, that He created all things out of nothing, and preserves them every moment, and could destroy them as easily as He made them; and that, in consequence, He is separated from them by an abyss, and is incommunicable in all His attributes.

And further, He has stamped upon all things, in the hour of their creation, their respective natures, and has given them their work and mission and their length of days, greater or less, in their appointed place. I mean, too, that He is ever present with His works, one by one, and confronts everything He has made by His particular and most loving Providence, and manifests Himself to each according to its needs; and has on rational beings imprinted the moral law, and given them power to obey it, imposing on them the duty of worship and service, searching and scanning them through and through with His omniscient eye, and putting before them a present trial and a judgment to come. Such is what Theology teaches about God. (*I. of U.*, p. 61ff.)

[THEOLOGY] teaches of a Being infinite, yet personal; all-blessed, yet ever operative; absolutely separate from the creature, yet in every part of the creation at every moment; above all things, yet under everything. It teaches of a Being who, though the highest, yet in the work of creation, conservation, government, retribution, makes Himself, as it were, the minister and servant of all; who, though inhabiting eternity, allows Himself to take an interest, and to have a sympathy, in the matters of space and time. His are all beings, visible and invisible, the noblest and the vilest of them. His are the substance, and the operation, and the results of that system of physical nature into which we are born. His too are the powers and achievements of the intellectual essences, on which He has bestowed an independent action and the gift of origination. The laws of the universe, the principles of truth, the relation of one thing to another, their qualities and virtues, the order and harmony of the whole, all that exists, is from Him; and, if evil is not from Him, as assuredly it is not, this is because evil has no substance of its own, but is only the defect, excess, perversion, or corruption of that which has substance. All we see, hear, and touch, the remote sidereal firmament, as well as our own sea and land, and the elements which compose them and the ordinances they obey, are His.

The primary atoms of matter, their properties, their mutual action, their disposition and collocation, electricity, magnetism, gravitation, light, and whatever other subtle principles or operations the wit of man is detecting or shall detect, are the work of His hands. From Him has been every movement which has convulsed and refashioned the surface of the earth. The most insignificant or unsightly insect is from Him, and good in its kind; the ever-teeming, inexhaustible swarms of animalculæ, the myriads of living motes invisible to the naked eye, the restless, ever-spreading vegetation which creeps like a garment over the whole earth, the lofty cedar, the umbrageous banana, are His. His are the tribes and families of birds and beasts, their graceful forms, their wild gestures, and their passionate cries. (*I. of U.*, p. 63ff.)

THE problem for statesmen of this age is how to educate the masses, and literature and science cannot give the solution. (*D. and A.*, p. 292)

MAN, with his motives and works, his languages, his propagation, his diffusion, is from God. Agriculture, medicine, and the arts of life, are His gifts. Society, laws, government, He is their sanction. The pageant of earthly royalty has the semblance and the benediction of the Eternal King. Peace and civilization, commerce and adventure, wars when just, conquest when humane and necessary, have His co-operation, and His blessing upon them. The course of events, the revolution of empires, the rise and fall of states, the periods and eras, the progresses and the retrogressions of the world's history, not indeed the incidental sin, over-abundant as it is, but the great outlines and the results of human affairs, are from His disposition. The elements and types and seminal principles and constructive powers of the moral world, in ruins though it be, are to be referred to Him.

He "enlighteneth every man that cometh into this world." His are the dictates of the moral sense, and the retributive reproaches of conscience. To Him must be ascribed the rich endowments of the intellect, the irradiation of genius, the imagination of the poet, the sagacity of the politician, the wisdom (as Scripture calls it), which now rears and decorates the Temple, now manifests itself in proverb or in parable. The old saws of nations, the majestic precepts of philosophy, the luminous maxims of law, the oracles of individual wisdom, the traditionary rules of truth, justice, and religion, even though imbedded in the corruption, or alloyed with the pride, of the world, betoken His original agency, and His long-suffering presence. (*I. of U.*, p. 64f.)

UNBELIEVERS call themselves rational; not because they decide by evidence, but because, after they have made their decision, they merely occupy themselves in sifting it. (*O. U. S.*, p. 230)

EVEN where there is habitual rebellion against God, or profound far-spreading social depravity, still the undercurrent, or the heroic outburst, of natural virtue, as well as the yearnings of the heart after what it has not, and its presentiment of its true remedies, are to be ascribed to the Author of all good. Anticipations or reminiscences of His glory haunt the mind of the self-sufficient sage, and of the pagan devotee; His writing is upon the wall, whether of the Indian fane, or of the porticoes of Greece.

He introduces Himself, He all but concurs, according to His good pleasure, and in His selected season, in the issues of unbelief, superstition, and false worship, and He changes the character of acts by His overruling operation. He condescends, though he gives no sanction, to the altars and shrines of imposture, and He makes His own fiat the substitute for its sorceries. He speaks amid the incantations of Balaam, raises Samuel's spirit in the witch's cavern, prophesies of the Messias by the tongue of the Sibyl, forces Python to recognize His ministers, and baptizes by the hand of the misbeliever. He is with the heathen dramatist in his denunciations of injustice and tyranny, and his auguries of divine vengeance upon crime.

Even on the unseemly legends of a popular mythology He casts His shadow, and is dimly discerned in the ode or the epic, as in troubled water or in fantastic dreams. All that is good, all that is true, all that is beautiful, all that is beneficent, be it great or small, be it perfect or fragmentary, natural as well as supernatural, moral as well as material, comes from Him. (*I. of U.*, p. 65f.)

WHEN men understand each other's meaning, they see, for the most part, that controversy is either superfluous or hopeless. (*O. U. S.*, p. 201)

CHRISTIANITY, and nothing short of it, must be made the element and principle of all education. Where it has been laid as the first stone, and acknowledged as the governing spirit, it will take up into itself, assimilate, and give a character to literature and science. Where Revealed Truth has given the aim and direction to Knowledge, Knowledge of all kinds will minister to Revealed Truth. But if in education we begin with nature before grace, with evidences before faith, with science before conscience, with poetry before practice, we shall be doing much the same as if we were to indulge the appetites and passions, and turn a deaf ear to the reason. In each case we misplace what in its place is a divine gift. If we attempt to effect a moral improvement by means of poetry, we shall but mature into a mawkish, frivolous, and fastidious sentimentalism;—if by means of argument, into a dry, unamiable longheadedness;—if by good society, into a polished outside, with hollowness within, in which vice has lost its grossness, and perhaps increased its malignity;—if by experimental science, into an uppish, supercilious temper much inclined to scepticism. But reverse the order of things: put Faith first and Knowledge second. (*D. and A.*, p. 274f.)

PEOPLE say to me, that it is but a dream to suppose that Christianity should regain the organic power in human society which once it possessed. I cannot help that; I never said it could. I am not a politician; I am proposing no measures, but exposing a fallacy, and resisting a pretence. Let Benthamism reign, if men have no aspirations; but do not tell them to be romantic, and then solace them with glory; do not attempt by philosophy what once was done by religion. The ascendancy of Faith may be impracticable, but the reign of Knowledge is incomprehensible. The problem for statesmen of this age is how to educate the masses, and literature and science cannot give the solution. (*D. and A.*, p. 292.)

SCIENCE gives us the grounds or premises from which religious truths are to be inferred; but it does not set about inferring them, much less does it reach the inference;—that is not its province. It brings before us phenomena, and it leaves us, if we will, to call them works of design, wisdom, or benevolence; and further still, if we will, to proceed to confess an Intelligent Creator. We have to take its facts, and to give them a meaning, and to draw our own conclusions from them. First comes Knowledge, then a view, then reasoning, and then belief. This is why Science has so little of a religious tendency; deductions have no power of persuasion. The heart is commonly reached, not through the reason, but through the imagination, by means of direct impressions, by the testimony of facts and events, by history, by description. Persons influence us, voices melt us, looks subdue us, deeds inflame us. Many a man will live and die upon a dogma: no man will be a martyr for a conclusion. (*D. and A.*, p. 292f.)

A LITERARY religion is so little to be depended upon; it looks well in fair weather, but its doctrines are opinions, and, when called to suffer for them, it slips them between its folios, or burns them at its hearth. (*D. and A.*, p. 293)

LOGIC makes but a sorry rhetoric with the multitude; first shoot round corners, and you may not despair of converting by a syllogism. Tell men to gain notions of a Creator from His works, and, if they were to set about it (which nobody does), they would be jaded and wearied by the labyrinth they were tracing. Their minds would be gorged and surfeited by the logical operation. Logicians are more set upon concluding rightly, than on right conclusions. They cannot see the end for the process. Few men have that power of mind which may hold fast and firmly a variety of thoughts. We ridicule "men of one idea"; but a great many of us are born to be such, and we should be happier if we knew it. To most men argument makes the point in hand only more doubtful, and considerably less impressive. After all, man is *not* a reasoning animal; he is a seeing, feeling, contemplating, acting animal. (*D. and A.*, p. 294)

ONE is not at all pleased when poetry, or eloquence, or devotion is considered as if chiefly intended to feed syllogisms. (*Apol.*, p. 265)

LIFE is not long enough for a religion of inferences; we shall never have done beginning, if we determine to begin with proof. We shall ever be laying our foundations; we shall turn theology into evidences, and divines into textuaries. We shall never get at our first principles. Resolve to believe nothing, and you must prove your proofs and analyze your elements, sinking further and further, and finding "in the lowest depth a lower deep," till you come to the broad bosom of scepticism. I would rather be bound to defend the reasonableness of assuming that Christianity is true, than to demonstrate a moral governance from the physical world. Life is for action. If we insist on proofs for everything, we shall never come to action: to act you must assume, and that assumption is faith.

Let no one suppose that in saying this I am maintaining that all proofs are equally difficult, and all propositions equally debatable. Some assumptions are greater than others, and some doctrines involve postulates larger than others, and more numerous. I only say that impressions lead to action, and that reasonings lead from it. Knowledge of premises, and inferences upon them,—this is not to *live*. It is very well as a matter of liberal curiosity and of philosophy to analyze our modes of thought; but let this come second, and when there is leisure for it, and then our examinations will in many ways even be subservient to action. But if we commence with scientific knowledge and argumentative proof, or lay any great stress upon it as the basis of personal Christianity, or attempt to make man moral and religious by Libraries and Museums, let us in consistency take chemists for our cooks, and mineralogists for our masons. (*D. and A.,* p. 295f.)

NO RELIGION has yet been a Religion of physics or of philosophy. It has ever been synonymous with Revelation. It never has been a deduction from what we know: it has ever been an assertion of what we are to believe. It has never lived in a conclusion; it has ever been a message, or a history, or a vision. No legislator or priest ever dreamed of educating our moral nature by science or by argument. There is no difference here between true Religions and pretended. Moses was instructed, not to reason from the creation, but to work miracles. Christianity is a history, supernatural, and almost scenic: it tells us what its Author is, by telling us what He has done. (*D. and A.*, p. 296)

I BELIEVE that the study of Nature, when religious feeling is away, leads the mind, rightly or wrongly, to acquiesce in the atheistic theory, as the simplest and easiest. It is but parallel to that tendency in anatomical studies, which no one will deny, to solve all the phenomena of the human frame into material elements and powers, and to dispense with the soul. To those who are conscious of matter, but not conscious of mind, it seems more rational to refer all things to one origin, such as they know, than to assume the existence of a second origin such as they know not. It is Religion, then, which suggests to Science its true conclusions; the facts come from Knowledge, but the principles come of Faith. (*D. and A.*, p. 300)

THE system of Nature is just as much connected with Religion, where minds are not religious, as a watch or a steam-carriage. The material world, indeed, is infinitely more wonderful than any human contrivance; but wonder is not religion, or we should be worshipping our railroads. What the physical creation presents to us in itself is a piece of machinery, and when men speak of a Divine Intelligence as its Author, this god of theirs is not the Living and True, unless the spring is the god of a watch, or steam the creator of the engine. Their idol, taken at advantage (though it is *not* an idol, for they do not worship it), is the animating principle of a vast and complicated system; it is subjected to laws, and it is connatural and co-extensive with matter. Well does Lord Brougham call it "the great architect of nature;" it is an instinct, or a soul of the world, or a vital power; it is not the Almighty God. (*D. and A.*, p. 302)

IT IS Rationalism to accept the Revelation and then to explain it away; to speak of it as the Word of God, and to treat it as the word of man; to refuse to let it speak for itself; to claim to be told the *why* and the *how* of God's dealings with us, as therein described, and to assign to Him a motive and scope of our own; to stumble at the partial knowledge which He may give us of them; to put aside what is obscure, as if it had not been said at all; to accept one half of what has been told us, and not the other half; to assume that the contents of Revelation are also its proof; to frame some gratuitous hypothesis about them, and then to garble, gloss, and colour them, to trim, clip, pare away, and twist them, in order to bring them into conformity with the idea to which we have subjected them.

Conduct such as this, on so momentous a matter, is, generally speaking, traceable to one obvious cause—the Rationalist makes himself his own centre, not his Maker; he does not go to God, but he implies that God must come to him. (*E. C. and H*. I. 32ff.)

WHAT an awful vitality is in the Catholic Church! What a heavenly-sustained sovereignty! What a self-evident divinity! She claims, she seeks, she desires no temporal power, no secular station; she meddles not with Cæsar or the things of Cæsar; she obeys him in his place,

but she is independent of him. Her strength is in her
God; her rule is over the souls of men; her glory is in
their willing subjection and loving loyalty. She hopes and
fears nothing from the world; it made her not, nor can
it destroy her. She can benefit it largely, but she does not
force herself upon it. She may be persecuted by it, but she
thrives under the persecution. She may be ignored, she
may be silenced and thrown into a corner, but she is
thought of the more. Calumniate her, and her influence
grows; ridicule her,—she does but smile upon you more
awfully and persuasively. What will you do with her, ye
sons of men, if you will not love her, if at least you will
not suffer her? Let the last three hundred years reply.
Let her alone, refrain from her; for if her counsel or her
work be of men, it will come to nought; but if it be of
God, you cannot overthrow it, lest perhaps you be found
even to fight against God. (*S. V. O.*, p. 137f.)

WHEN the awful form of Catholicism, of which [the
present day Englishman] has already heard so much good
and so much evil—so much evil which revolts him, so
much good which amazes and troubles him—when this
great vision, which hitherto he has known from books
and from rumour, but not by sight and hearing, presents
itself before him, it finds in him a very different being
from the simple Anglo-Saxon to whom it originally came.
It finds in him a being, not of rude nature, but of formed
habits, averse to change and resentful of interference; a
being who looks hard at it, and repudiates and loathes
it, first of all, because, if listened to, it would give him
much trouble. He wishes to be let alone; but here is a
teaching which purports to be revealed, which would
mould his mind on new ideas, which he has to learn, and

which, if he cannot learn thoroughly, he must borrow from strangers.

The very notion of a theology or a ritual frightens and oppresses him; it is a yoke, because it makes religion difficult, not easy. There is enough of labour in learning matters of this life, without concerning oneself with the revelations of another. He does not choose to believe that the Almighty has told us so many things, and he readily listens to any person or argument maintaining the negative. And, moreover, he resents the idea of interference itself; "an Englishman's house is his castle;" a maxim most salutary in politics, most dangerous in moral conduct. He cannot bear the thought of not having a will of his own, or an opinion of his own, on any given subject of enquiry, whatever it be. It is intolerable, as he considers, not to be able, on the most awful and difficult of subjects, to think for oneself; it is an insult to be told that God has spoken and superseded investigation.

The more [men of this type] see of the members [of the Catholic Church] the more their worst suspicions are confirmed. They did not wish, they say, to believe the popular notions of her anti-Christian character; but, really, after what they have seen of her authorities and her people, nothing is left to them but an hostility to her, which they are loth to adopt. They wish to think the best of every one, but this ecclesiastical measure, that speech, that book, those persons, those expressions, that line of thought, those realized results, all tend one way, and force them to unlearn a charitableness which is as pernicious as it is illusory.

Thus they speak; alas, they do not see that they are assuming the very point in dispute; for the original question is, whether Catholics or they are right in their respective principles and views, and to decide it merely

by what is habitual to themselves is to exercise the double
office of accuser and judge. Yet multitudes of sober and
serious minds and well-regulated lives look out upon the
Catholic Church and shrink back again from her presence, on no better reasons than these.

They cannot endure her; their whole being revolts from
her; she leaves, as they speak, a bad taste in their mouths;
all is so novel, so strange, so unlike what is familiar to
them, so unlike the Anglican Prayer-Book, so unlike some
favourite author of their own, so different from what they
would do or say themselves, requires so much explanation, is so strained and unnatural, so unreal and extravagant, so unquiet, nay, so disingenuous, so unfeeling, that
they cannot even tolerate it. The Mass is so difficult to
follow, and we say prayers so very quickly, and we sit
when we should stand, and we talk so freely when we
should be reserved, and we keep Sunday so differently
from them, and we have such notions of our own about
marriage and celibacy, and we approve of vows, and we
class virtues and sins on so unreasonable a standard;
these and a thousand such details are, in the case of numbers, decisive proofs that we deserve the hard names
which are heaped on us by the world.

They do not judge of us by the rules they apply to
the conduct of themselves and each other; what they
praise or allow in those they admire is an offence to
them in us. Day by day, then, as it passes, furnishes,
as a matter of course, a series of charges against us,
simply because it furnishes a succession of our sayings
and doings. Whatever we do, whatever we do not do, is
a demonstration against us. Do we argue? men are surprised at our insolence or effrontery. Are we silent? we
are underhand and deep. Do we appeal to the law? it is
in order to evade it. Do we obey the Church? it is a sign

of our disloyalty. Do we state our pretensions? we blaspheme. Do we conceal them? we are liars and hypocrites. Do we display the pomp of our ceremonial, and the habits of our Religious? our presumption has become intolerable. Do we put them aside and dress as others? we are ashamed of being seen, and skulk about as conspirators.

Not a word that we say, not a deed that we do, but is viewed in the medium of that one idea, by the light of that one prejudice, which our enemies cherish concerning us; not a word or a deed but is grafted on the original assumption that we certainly come from below, and are the servants of Antichrist. (*S. V. O.*, p. 150ff.)

PROTESTANTS actually set up images to represent their heroes, and they show them honour without any misgiving. The very flower and cream of Protestantism used to glory in the statue of King William, on College Green, Dublin; and I recollect well what a shriek they raised some years ago, when the figure was unhorsed. Some profane person one night applied gunpowder, and blew the King right out of his saddle, and he was found by those who took interest in him, like Dagon, on the ground. You might have thought the poor senseless block had life to see the way people took on about it, and how they spoke of his face, and his arms, and his legs; yet those same Protestants, I say, would at the same time be horrified had I used "he" and "him" of a crucifix, and would call me one of the monsters described in the Apocalypse did I but honour my living Lord as they their dead King. (*P. P. C.*, p. 181.)

WHAT is invidiously called dogmatism and system, in one shape or other, in one degree or another, is necessary to the human mind. (*O. U. S.*, p. 297)

DID St. Athanasius or St. Ambrose come suddenly to life, it cannot be doubted what communion he would take to be his own. All surely will agree that these Fathers, with whatever opinions of their own, whatever protests, if we will, would find themselves more at home with such men as St. Bernard or St. Ignatius Loyola, or with the lonely priest in his lodging, or the holy sisterhood of mercy, or the unlettered crowd before the altar, than with the teachers or with the members of any other creed. And may we not add, that were those same Saints who once sojourned, one in exile, one on embassy, at Treves, to come more northward still, and to travel until they reached another fair city, seated among groves, green meadows and calm streams, the holy brothers would turn from many a high aisle and solemn cloister which they found there, and ask the way to some small chapel where mass was said in the populous alley or forlorn suburb? (*D. Ch. D.*, p. 97f.)

IT IS considered, and justly, as an evidence for Christianity, that the ablest men have been Christians; not that all sagacious or profound minds have taken up its profession, but that it has gained victories among them, such and so many, as to show that it is not the mere fact of ability or learning which is the reason why all are not converted. Such, too, is the characteristic of Catholicity; not the highest in rank, not the meanest, not the most refined, not the rudest, is beyond the influence of the Church; she includes specimens of every class among her children.

She is the solace of the forlorn, the chastener of the prosperous and the guide of the wayward. She keeps a mother's eye for the innocent, bears with a heavy hand upon the wanton and has a voice of majesty for the proud. She opens the mind of the ignorant, and she prostrates the intellect of even the most gifted. These are not words; she has done it, she does it still, she undertakes to do it. All she asks is an open field, and freedom to act. She asks no patronage from the civil power: in former times and places she indeed has asked it; and, as Protestantism also, has availed herself of the civil sword.

It is true she did so, because in certain ages it has been the acknowledged mode of acting, the most expeditious, and open at the time to no objection, and because, where she has done so, the people clamoured for it and did it in advance of her; but her history shows that she needed it not, for she has extended and flourished without it. She is ready for any service which occurs; she will take the world as it comes; nothing but force can repress her.

See, my brethren, what she is doing in [England] now;* for three centuries the civil power has trodden down the goodly plant of grace, and kept its foot upon it; at length circumstances have removed that tyranny, and lo! the fair form of the Ancient Church rises up at once, as fresh and as vigorous as if she had never intermitted her growth. She is the same as she was three centuries ago, ere the present religions of the country existed; you know her to be the same; it is the charge brought against her that she does not change; time and place affect her not, because she has her source where there is neither place nor time, because she comes from the throne of the Illimitable, Eternal God. (*D. M. C.*, p. 252ff.)

[THE Blessed Virgin] died in private. It became Him, who died for the world, to die in the world's sight; it became the Great Sacrifice to be lifted up on high, as a

* 1849.

light that could not be hid. But she, the Lily of Eden, who had always dwelt out of the sight of man, fittingly did she die in the garden's shade, and amid the sweet flowers in which she had lived. Her departure made no noise in the world. The Church went about her common duties, preaching, converting, suffering. There were persecutions, there was fleeing from place to place, there were martyrs, there were triumphs. At length the rumour spread abroad that the Mother of God was no longer upon earth. Pilgrims went to and fro; they sought for her relics, but they found them not; did she die at Ephesus? or did she die at Jerusalem? reports varied; but her tomb could not be pointed out, or if it was found, it was open; and instead of her pure and fragrant body, there was a growth of lilies from the earth which she had touched. (*D. M. C.*, p. 373)

THE Prejudiced Man takes it for granted, or feels an undoubting persuasion,—not only that he himself is in possession of divine truth, for this is a matter of opinion, and he has a right to his own,—but that we, who differ from him, are universally impostors, tyrants, hypocrites, cowards, and slaves. This is a first principle with him; it is like divine faith in the Catholic, nothing can shake it. If he meets with any story against Catholics, on any or no authority, which does but fall in with this notion of them, he eagerly catches at it. Authority goes for nothing; likelihood, as he considers it, does instead of testimony; what he is now told is just what he expected.

Perhaps it is a random report, put into circulation merely because it has a chance of succeeding, or thrown like a straw to the wind: perhaps it is a mere publisher's speculation, who thinks that a narrative of horrors will

pay well for the printing: it matters not, he is perfectly
convinced of its truth; he knew all about it beforehand;
it is just what he always has said; it is the old tale over
again a hundred times. Accordingly he buys it by the
thousand, and sends it about with all speed in every
direction, to his circle of friends and acquaintance, to the
newspapers, to the great speakers at public meetings;
he fills the Sunday and week-day schools with it; loads
the pedlars' baskets, perhaps introduces it into the family
spiritual reading on Sunday evenings, consoled and comforted with the reflection that he has got something fresh
and strong and undeniable, in evidence of the utter
odiousness of the Catholic Religion. (*P. P. C.*, p. 236f.)

IF A person ventures to ask the Prejudiced Man what
he knows of Catholics personally—what he knows of individuals, of their ways, of their books, or of their
worship, he blesses himself that he knows nothing of them
at all, and he never will; nay, if they fall in his way, he
will take himself out of it; and if unawares he shall ever
be pleased with a Catholic without knowing who it is,
he wishes by anticipation to retract such feeling of pleasure. About our state of mind, our views of things, our
ends and objects, our doctrines, our defence of them, our
judgment on his objections to them, our thoughts about
him, he absolutely refuses to be enlightened: and he is as
sore if expostulated with on so evident an infirmity of
mind, as if it were some painful wound upon him, or local
inflammation, which must not be handled ever so tenderly. He shrinks from the infliction.

However, one cannot always make the whole world
take one's own way of thinking; so let us suppose the
famous story, to which the Prejudiced Man has pledged

his veracity, utterly discredited and scattered to the winds by the common consent of mankind:—this only makes him the more violent. For it *ought*, he thinks, to be true, and it is mere special pleading to lay much stress on its not having all the evidence which it might have; for if it be not true, yet half a hundred like stories are. It is only impertinent to ask for evidence, when the fact has so often been established. What is the good of laboriously vindicating St. Eligius, or exposing a leading article in a newspaper, or a speaker at a meeting, or a popular publication, when the thing is notorious; and to deny it is nothing else than a vexatious demand upon his time, and an insult to his common sense. He is but enraged so much the more, and almost put beside himself, by the presumption of those who, with their doubts or their objections, interfere with the great Protestant Tradition about the Catholic Church.

To bring proof against us is, he thinks, but a matter of time; and we know in affairs of every day, how annoyed and impatient we are likely to become, when obstacles are put in our way in any such case. We are angered at delays when they are but accidental, and the issue is certain; we are not angered, but we are sobered, we become careful and attentive to impediments, when there is a doubt about the issue. The very same difficulties put us on our mettle in the one case, and do but irritate us in the other. If, for instance, a person cannot open a door, or get a key into a lock, which he has done a hundred times before, you know how apt he is to shake, and to rattle, and to force it, as if some great insult was offered him by its resistance: you know how surprised a wasp, or other large insect is, that he cannot get through a window-pane; such is the feeling of the Prejudiced Man, when we urge our objections—not softened by them at all, but exasperated the more; for what is the use of even incontrovertible arguments against a conclusion which he already considers to be infallible? (*P. P. C.*, p. 238ff.)

WE WILL suppose [the Prejudiced Man] in a specially good humour, when you set about undeceiving him on some point on which he misstates the Catholic faith. He is determined to be candour and fairness itself, and to do full justice to your argument. So you begin your explanation; you assure him he misconceives your doctrines; he has got a wrong view of facts. You appeal to original authorities, and show him how shamefully they have been misquoted; you appeal to history and prove it has been garbled. Nothing is wanted to your representation; it is triumphant. He is silent for a moment, then he begins with a sentiment. "What clever fellows these Catholics are!" he says, "I defy you to catch them tripping; they have a way out of everything. I thought we had you, but I fairly own I am beaten. This is how the Jesuits got on; always educated, subtle, well up in their books; a Protestant has no chance with them." You see you have not advanced a step in convincing him. (*P. P. C.*, p. 241.)

THE Prejudiced Man [is often] grave and suspicious. "I confess," he will say, "I do *not* like these very complete explanations; they are too like a made-up case. I can easily believe there was exaggeration in the charge; perhaps money was only sometimes taken for the permission to sin, or only before the Reformation, but our friend professes to prove it never was taken; this is proving too much. I always suspect something behind, when every-

thing is so very easy and clear." Or again, "We see before
our eyes a tremendous growth of Popery; *how* does it
grow? You tell me you are poor, your priests few, your
friends without influence; then how does it *grow?* It could
not grow without means! it is bad enough if you can
assign a cause; it is worse if you cannot. Cause there
must be somewhere, for effects imply causes. How did it
get into Oxford? tell me that. How has it got among
the Protestant clergy? I like all things above board; I
hate concealment, I detest plots. There is evidently something to be accounted for; and the more cogently you
prove that it is not referable to anything which we see,
the graver suspicions do you awaken, that it is traceable
to something which is hidden."

Thus our Prejudiced Man simply ignores the possible
existence of that special cause to which Catholics of
course refer the growth of Catholicism, and which surely,
if admitted, is sufficient to account for it—viz., that it is
true. He will not admit the power of truth among the
assignable conjectural causes. He would rather, I am
sure, assign it to the agency of evil spirits, than suspect
the possibility of a religion being true which he wills
should be a falsehood. (*P. P. C.*, p., 242f.)

UNITARIANS, Sabellians, Utilitarians, Wesleyans, Cal-
vinists, Swedenborgians, Irvingites, Freethinkers, all
these [the Church of England] can tolerate in its very
bosom; no form of opinion comes amiss; but Rome it
cannot abide. It agrees to differ with its own children on
a thousand points, one is sacred—that her Majesty the
Queen is "The Mother and Mistress of all Churches;" on
one dogma it is infallible, on one it may securely insist
without fear of being unseasonable or excessive—that "the

Bishop of Rome hath no jurisdiction in this realm." Here is sunshine amid the darkness, sense amid confusion, an intelligible strain amid a Babel of sounds; whatever befalls, here is sure footing; it is, "No peace with Rome," "Down with the Pope," and "The Church in danger."

Never has the Establishment failed in the use of these important and effective watchwords; many are its shortcomings, but it is without reproach in the execution of this its special charge. Heresy, and scepticism, and infidelity, and fanaticism, may challenge it in vain; but fling upon the gale the faintest whisper of Catholicism, and it recognizes by instinct the presence of its connatural foe. Forthwith, as during the last year, the atmosphere is tremulous with agitation, and discharges its vibrations far and wide. A movement is in birth which has no natural crisis or resolution.

Spontaneously the bells of the steeples begin to sound. Not by an act of volition, but by a sort of mechanical impulse, bishop and dean, archdeacon and canon, rector and curate, one after another, each on his high tower, off they set, swinging and booming, tolling and chiming, with nervous intenseness, and thickening emotion, and deepening volume, the old ding-dong which has scared town and country this weary time; tolling and chiming away, jingling and clamouring and ringing the changes on their poor half-dozen notes, all about "the Popish aggression," "insolent and insidious," "insidious and insolent," "insolent and atrocious," "atrocious and insolent," "atrocious, insolent, and ungrateful," "ungrateful, insolent, and atrocious," "foul and offensive," "pestilent and horrid," "subtle and unholy," "audacious and revolting," "contemptible and shameless," "malignant," "frightful," "mad," "meretricious,"—bobs (I think the ringers call them), bobs, and bobs-royal, and triple-bob-majors, and grandsires,—to the extent of their compass and the full ring of their metal, in honour of Queen Bess, and to the confusion of the Holy Father and the Princes of the Church. (*P. P. C.*, p. 75ff.)

BIGOTRY is the infliction of our own unproved First Principles on others, and the treating others with scorn or hatred for not accepting them. It is not bigotry to despise intemperance; it is not bigotry to hate injustice or cruelty; but whatever is local, or national, or sectional, or personal, or novel, and nothing more, to make that the standard of judging all existing opinions, without an attempt at proving it to be of authority, is mere ridiculous bigotry. *"In necessariis unitas, in dubiis libertas,"* is ever the rule of a true philosopher. And though I know in many cases it is very difficult to draw the line, and to decide what principles are, and what are not, independent of individuals, times and places, eternal and divine, yet so far we may safely assert,—that when the very persons who hold certain views, confess, nay, boast, nay, are jealously careful, that those views come of their own private judgment, they at least should be as jealous and as careful to keep them to their own place, and not to use them as if they came distinctly from heaven, or from the nature of things, or from the nature of man. Those persons, surely, are precluded, if they would be consistent, from using their principles as authoritative, who proclaim that they made them for themselves. (*P. P. C.*, p. 292f.)

THERE is much need of wariness, jealousy of self, and habitual dread of presumption, paradox, and unreality, to preserve our guesses from assuming the character of discoveries. (*O. U. S.*, p. 295)

CATHOLICISM has its First Principles; overthrow them, if you can; endure them, if you cannot. It is not enough to call them effete because they are old, or antiquated because they are ancient. It is not enough to look into our churches, and cry, "It is all a form, *because* divine favour cannot depend on external observances;" or, "It is all a bondage, *because* there is no such thing as sin;" or, "a blasphemy, *because* the Supreme Being cannot be present in ceremonies;" or, "a mummery, *because* prayer cannot move Him;" or, "a tyranny, *because* vows are unnatural;" or, "hypocrisy, *because* no rational man can credit it at all." I say here is endless assumption, unmitigated hypothesis, reckless assertion; prove your "because," "because," "because;" prove your First Principles, and if you cannot, learn philosophic moderation.

Why may not my First Principles contest the prize with yours? they have been longer in the world; they have lasted longer, they have done harder work, they have seen rougher service. You sit in your easy-chairs, you dogmatize in your lecture-rooms, you wield your pens: it all looks well on paper: you write exceedingly well: there never was an age in which there was better writing; logical, nervous, eloquent, and pure,—go and carry it all out in the world.

Take your First Principles, of which you are so proud, into the crowded streets of our cities, into the formidable classes which make up the bulk of our population; try to work society by them. You think you can; I say you cannot—at least you have not as yet; it is yet to be seen if you can. "Let not him that putteth on his armour boast as he who taketh it off." Do not take it for granted that that is certain which is waiting the test of reason and experiment. Be modest until you are victorious.

My principles, which I believe to be eternal, have at

least lasted eighteen hundred years; let yours live as many months. That man can sin, that he has duties, that the Divine Being hears prayer, that He gives His favours through visible ordinances, that He is really present in the midst of them, these principles have been the life of nations; they have shown they could be carried out; let any single nation carry out yours, and you will have better claim to speak contemptuously of Catholic rites, of Catholic devotions, of Catholic belief. (*P. P. C.*, p. 294f.)

STARTING with the being of a God (which, as I have said, is as certain to me as the certainty of my own existence, though when I try to put the grounds of that certainty into logical shape I find a difficulty in doing so in mood and figure to my satisfaction) I look out of myself into the world of men, and there I see a sight which fills me with unspeakable distress. The world seems simply to give the lie to that great truth, of which my whole being is so full; and the effect upon me is, in consequence, as a matter of necessity, as confusing as if it denied that I am in existence myself.

If I looked into a mirror and did not see my face, I should have the sort of feeling which actually comes upon me when I look into this living busy world and see no reflection of its Creator. This is, to me, one of those great difficulties of this absolute primary truth to which I referred just now. Were it not for this voice speaking so clearly in my conscience and my heart, I should be an atheist, or a pantheist, or a polytheist when I looked into the world. I am speaking for myself only; and I am far from denying the real force of the arguments in proof of a God, drawn from the general facts of human society and the course of history; but these do not warm me or enlighten me; they do not take away the winter of my desolation, or make the buds unfold and the leaves grow within me and my moral being rejoice. The sight of the world is nothing else than the prophet's scroll, full of "lamentations, and mourning, and woe."

To consider the world in its length and breadth, its various history, the many races of man, their starts, their fortunes, their mutual alienation, their conflicts; and then their ways, habits, governments, forms of worship; their enterprises, their aimless courses, their random achievements and acquirements, the impotent conclusion of long-standing facts, the tokens so faint and broken of a superintending design, the blind evolution of what turn out to be great powers or truths, the progress of things, as if from unreasoning elements, not towards final causes, the greatness and littleness of man, his far-reaching aims, his short duration, the curtain hung over his futurity, the disappointments of life, the defeat of good, the success of evil, physical pain, mental anguish, the prevalence and intensity of sin, the pervading idolatries, the corruptions, the dreary hopeless irreligion, that condition of the whole race so fearfully yet exactly described in the Apostle's words, "having no hope and without God in the world,"—all this is a vision to dizzy and appal; and inflicts upon the mind the sense of a profound mystery which is absolutely beyond human solution.

What shall be said to this heart-piercing, reason-bewildering fact? I can only answer, that either there is no Creator, or this living society of men is in a true sense discarded from His presence. Did I see a boy of good make and mind, with the tokens on him of a refined nature, cast upon the world without provision, unable to say whence he came, his birthplace or his family connections, I should conclude that there was some mystery connected with his history, and that he was one of whom, from one cause or other, his parents were ashamed. Thus only should I be able to account for the contrast between the promise and the condition of his being. And so I argue about the world;—*if* there be a God, *since* there is a God, the human race is implicated in some terrible aboriginal calamity. It is out of joint with the purposes of its Creator. This is a fact—a fact as true as the fact of its existence; and thus the doctrine of what is theologically called original sin becomes to me almost as certain as that the world exists, and as the existence of God.

And now, supposing it were the blessed and loving will of the Creator to interfere in this anarchical condition of things, what are we to suppose would be the methods which might be necessarily or naturally involved in His purpose of mercy? Since the world is in so abnormal a state, surely it would be no surprise to me if the interposition were of necessity equally extraordinary —or what is called miraculous. But that subject does not directly come into the scope of my present remarks. Miracles, as evidence, involve a process of reason or an argument; and of course I am thinking of some mode of interference which does not immediately run into argument. I am rather asking what must be the face-to-face antagonist by which to withstand and baffle the fierce energy of passion and the all-corroding, all-dissolving scepticism of the intellect in religious inquiries?

I have no intention at all of denying that truth is the real object of our reason, and that, if it does not attain to truth, either the premiss or the process is in fault; but I am not speaking here of right reason, but of reason as it acts in fact and concretely in fallen man. I know that even the unaided reason, when correctly exercised, leads to a belief in God, in the immortality of the soul, and in a future retribution; but I am considering the faculty of reason actually and historically; and in this point of view I do not think I am wrong in saying that its tendency is towards a simple unbelief in matters of religion. No truth, however sacred, can stand against it, in the long run; and hence it is that in the pagan world, when our Lord came, the last traces of the religious knowledge of former times were all but disappearing from those portions of the world in which the intellect had been active and had had a career.

And in these latter days, in like manner, outside the Catholic Church things are tending—with far greater rapidity than in that old time from the circumstance of the age—to atheism in one shape or other. What a scene, what a prospect, does the whole of Europe present at this day! and not only Europe, but every government and every civilization through the world, which is under the influence of the European mind! Lovers of their country and of their race, religious men, external to the Catholic Church, have attempted various expedients to arrest fierce wilful human nature in its onward course, and to bring it into subjection. The necessity of some form of religion for the interests of humanity has been generally acknowledged: but where was the concrete representative of things invisible, which would have the force and the toughness necessary to be a breakwater against the deluge?

Three centuries ago the establishment of religion, material, legal, and social, was generally adopted as the best expedient for the purpose in those countries which separated from the Catholic Church; and for a long time it was successful; but now the crevices of those establishments are admitting the enemy. Thirty years ago education was relied upon: then years ago there was a hope that wars would cease for ever, under the influence of commercial enterprise and the reign of the useful and fine arts; but will any one venture to say that there is any thing any where on this earth which will afford a fulcrum for us whereby to keep the earth from moving onwards?

The judgment which experience passes, whether on establishments or on education, as a means of maintaining religious truth in this anarchical world, must be extended even to Scripture, though Scripture be divine. Experience proves surely that the Bible does not answer a purpose for which it was never intended. It may be accidentally the means of the conversion of individuals: but a book, after all, cannot make a stand against the wild living intellect of man, and in this day it begins to testify, as regards its own structure and contents, to the power of that universal solvent which is so successfully acting upon religious establishments.

Supposing then it to be the Will of the Creator to interfere in human affairs, and to make provisions for retaining in the world a knowledge of Himself so definite and distinct as to be proof against the energy of human scepticism, in such a case—I am far from saying that there was no other way—but there is nothing to surprise the mind, if He should think fit to introduce a power into the world invested with the prerogative of infallibility in religious matters.

Such a provision would be a direct, immediate, active, and prompt means of withstanding the difficulty; it would be an instrument suited to the need; and when I find that this is the very claim of the Catholic Church, not only do I feel no difficulty in admitting the idea, but there is a fitness in it which recommends it to my mind. And thus

I am brought to speak of the Church's infallibility as a provision adapted by the mercy of the Creator to preserve religion in the world, and to restrain that freedom of thought which of course in itself is one of the greatest of our natural gifts, and to rescue it from its own suicidal excesses. (*Apol.*, p. 333ff.)

MIRACLES are not only not unlikely, they are positively likely; and for this simple reason, because, for the most part, when God begins He goes on. We conceive that when He first did a miracle, He began a series; what He commenced, He continued: what has been, will be. Surely this is good and clear reasoning. To my own mind, certainly, it is incomparably more difficult to believe that the Divine Being should do one miracle and no more, than that He should do a thousand; that He should do one great miracle only, than that He should do a multitude of less besides. This beautiful world of nature, His own work, He broke its harmony; He broke through His own laws which He had imposed on it; He worked out His purposes, not simply through it, but in violation of it. If He did this only in the lifetime of the Apostles, if He did it but once, eigtheen hundred years ago and more, that isolated infringement looks as the mere infringement of a rule: if Divine Wisdom would not leave an infringement, an anomaly, a solecism on His work, He might be expected to introduce a series of miracles, and turn the apparent exception into an additional law of His Providence. If the Divine Being does a thing once, He is, judging by human reason, likely to do it again. This surely is common sense.

Suppose you yourselves were once to see a miracle, would you not feel that experience to be like passing a line? should you, in consequence of it, declare, "I never will believe another if I hear of one"? would it not, on the contrary, predispose you to listen to a new report? would you scoff at it and call it priestcraft for the reason that you had actually seen one with your own eyes? I think you would not; then I ask what is the difference of the argument, whether you have seen one or believe one? You believe the Apostolic miracles, therefore be inclined beforehand to believe later ones. Thus you see, our First Principle, that miracles are not unlikely now, is not at all a strange one in the mouths of those who believe that the Supreme Being came miraculously into this world, miraculously united Himself to man's nature, passed a life of miracles and then gave His Apostles a greater gift of miracles than He exercised Himself. (*P. P. C.*, p. 306f.)

THERE are two systems going on in the world, one of nature, and one above nature; and two histories, one of common events, and one of miracles; and each system and each history has its own order. When I hear of the miracle of a Saint, my first feeling would be of the same kind as if it were a report of any natural exploit or event. Supposing, for instance, I heard a report of the death of some public man; it would not startle me, even if I did not at once credit it, for all men must die. Did I read of any great feat of valor, I should believe it, if imputed to Alexander or Cœur de Lion. Did I hear of any act of baseness, I should disbelieve it, if imputed to a friend whom I knew and loved.

Were a miracle reported to me as wrought by a member of Parliament, or a Bishop of the Establishment, or a Wesleyan preacher, I should repudiate the notion: were

it referred to a saint, or the relic of a saint, or the inter-
cession of a saint, I should not be startled at it, though
I might not at once believe it. And I certainly should be
right in this conduct, supposing my First Principle be
true. Miracles to the Catholic are facts of history and
biography, and nothing else; and they are to be regarded and dealt with as other facts; and as natural facts,
under circumstances, do not startle Protestants, so supernatural, under circumstances, do not startle the Catholic.
They may or may not have taken place in particular
cases; he may be unable to determine which; he may
have no distinct evidence; he may suspend his judgment,
but he will say, "It is very possible;" he never will say,
"I cannot believe it." (*P. P. C.*, p. 307f.)

o WISDOM of the world! and strength of the world!
what are you when matched beside the foolishness and
the weakness of the Christian? You are great in resources, manifold in methods, hopeful in prospects; but
one thing you have not,—and that is peace. You are always tumultuous, restless, apprehensive. You have nothing you can rely upon. You have no rock under your
feet. But the humblest, feeblest Christian has that which
is impossible to you. (*Cal.*, p. 353f.)

IT IS not at all easy (humanly speaking) to wind up an
Englishman to a dogmatic level. (*Apol.*, p. 296)

THE world believes in the world's ends as the greatest
of goods; it wishes society to be governed simply and
entirely for the sake of this world. Provided it could gain
one little islet in the ocean, one foot upon the coast, if it

could cheapen tea by sixpence a pound, or make its flag respected among the Esquimaux or Otaheitans, at the cost of a hundred lives and a hundred souls, it would think it a very good bargain. What does it know of hell? it disbelieves it; it spits upon it, abominates it, curses its very name and notion. Next, as to the devil, it does not believe in him either. We next come to the flesh, and it is "free to confess" that it does not think there is any great harm in following the instincts of that nature which, perhaps it goes on to say, God has given.

How could it be otherwise? who ever heard of the world fighting against the flesh and the devil? Well, then, what is its notion of evil? Evil, says the world, is whatever is an offence to me, whatever obscures my majesty, whatever disturbs my peace. Order, tranquillity, popular contentment, plenty, prosperity, advance in arts and sciences, literature, refinement, splendour—this is my millennium. I acknowledge no whole, no individuality, but my own; the units which compose me are but parts of me; they have no perfection in themselves; no end but in me; in my glory is their bliss, and in the hidings of my countenance they come to naught.

Such is the philosophy and practice of the world: now the Church looks and moves in a simply opposite direction (*A. D.* i. 235f.)

THE Church aims, not at making a show, but at doing a work. She regards this world, and all that is in it, as a mere shadow, as dust and ashes, compared with the value of one single soul. She holds that, unless she can, in her own way, do good to souls, it is no use her doing anything; she holds that it were better for sun and moon to drop from heaven, for the earth to fail, and for all the many millions who are upon it to die of starvation in extremest agony, so far as temporal affliction goes, than that one soul, I will not say, should be lost, but should commit one single venial sin, should tell one wilful untruth, though it harmed no one, or steal one poor farthing without excuse. She considers the action of this world and the action of the soul simply incommensurate, viewed in their respective spheres; she would rather save the soul of one single wild bandit of Calabria, or whining beggar of Palermo, than draw a hundred lines of railroad through the length and breadth of Italy, or carry out a sanitary reform, in its fullest details, in every city of Sicily, except so far as these great national works tended to some spiritual good beyond them. (*A. D.* i. 239f.)

THERE are seven notes in the [musical] scale; make them thirteen; yet what a slender outfit for so vast an enterprise! What science brings so much out of so little! Out of what poor elements does some great master in it create his new world! Shall we say that all this exuberant inventiveness is a mere ingenuity or trick of art, like some game or fashion of the day, without reality, without meaning? We may do so, and then perhaps we shall also account the science of theology to be a matter of words; yet, as there is a divinity in the theology of the Church which those who feel cannot communicate, so is there also in the wonderful creation of sublimity and beauty of which I am speaking.

To many men the very names which the science employs are utterly incomprehensible. To speak of an "idea" or a "subject" seems to be fanciful or trifling, and of the views which it opens upon us to be childish extravagance; yet is it possible that that inexhaustible evolution

and disposition of notes, so rich yet so simple, so intri‑
cate and yet so regulated, so various yet so majestic,
should be a mere sound which is gone and perishes?
Can it be that those mysterious stirrings of heart and keen
emotions and strange yearnings after we know not what
and awful impressions from we know not whence, should
be wrought in us by what is unsubstantial and comes and
goes and begins and ends in itself? It is not so; it cannot
be. No! they have escaped from some higher sphere:
they are the voice of angels or the magnificat of saints,
or the living laws of divine governance or the divine
attributes: something are they besides themselves which
we cannot compass, which we cannot utter; though mor‑
tal man, and he perhaps not otherwise distinguished
above his fellows, has the gift of eliciting them. (*O. U. S.,*
p. 346f.)

ALL IS dreary till we believe—what our hearts tell us—
that we are subjects of God's governance; nothing is
dreary, all inspires hope and trust, directly we under‑
stand that we are under His hand, and that whatever
comes to us is from Him as a method of discipline and
guidance. What is it to us whether the knowledge He
gives us be greater or less, if it be He who gives it? What
is it to us whether it be exact or vague, if He bids us
trust it? What have we to care whether we are or are
not given to divide substance from shadow, if He is
training us heavenwards by means of either? (*O. U. S.,*
p. 348)

EACH pursuit or calling has its own dangers, and each
numbers among its professors men who rise superior to
them. (*D. and A.,* p. 299)

WHEN the eyes of the infant first open upon the world, the reflected rays of light which strike them from the myriad of surrounding objects present to him no image but a medley of colours and shadows. They do not form into a whole; they do not rise into foregrounds and melt into distances; they do not divide into groups; they do not coalesce into unities; they do not combine into persons; but each particular hue and tint stands by itself, wedged in amid a thousand others upon the vast and flat mosaic, having no intelligence and conveying no story any more than the wrong side of some rich tapestry. The little babe stretches out his arms and fingers as if to grasp or to fathom the many-coloured vision; and thus he gradually learns the connexion of part with part, separates what moves from what is stationary, watches the coming and going of figures, masters the idea of shape and of perspective, calls in the information conveyed through the other senses to assist him in his mental process, and thus gradually converts a kaleidoscope into a picture. The first view was the more splendid, the second the more real; the former more poetical, the latter more philosophical. Alas! what are we doing all through life, both as a necessity, and as a duty, but unlearning the world's poetry and attaining to its prose? (*I. of U.*, p. 331f.)

ONE main portion of intellectual education, of the labours of both school and university is to remove the original dimness of the mind's eye; to strengthen and perfect its vision; to enable it to look out into the world right forward, steadily and truly; to give the mind clearness, accuracy, and precision; to enable it to use words aright, to understand what it says, to conceive justly what it thinks about, to abstract, compare, analyse, divide, define and reason, corectly. (*I. of U.*, p. 332)

AN INTELLECTUAL man, as the world now conceives of him, is one who is full of "views" on all subjects of philosophy, on all matters of the day. It is almost thought a disgrace not to have a view at a moment's notice on any question from the Personal Advent to the Cholera or Mesmerism. This is owing in great measure to the necessities of periodical literature now so much in request. Every quarter of a year, every month, every day there must be a supply, for the gratification of the public, of new and luminous theories on the subjects of religion, foreign politics, home politics, civil economy, finance, trade, agriculture, emigration, and the colonies. [These] must all be practised on, day after day, by what are called original thinkers. As the great man's guest must produce his good stories or songs at the evening banquet, as the platform orator exhibits his telling facts at midday, so the journalist lies under the stern obligation of extemporising his lucid views, leading ideas and nutshell truths for the breakfast-table. The very nature of periodical literature, broken into small wholes, and demanded punctually to an hour, involves the habit of this *extempore* philosophy. There is a demand for a reckless originality of thought and a sparkling plausibility of argument: a demand for crude theory and unsound philosophy rather than none at all. (*I. of U.*, p. xxf.)

WHILE the many use language as they find it, the man of genius uses it indeed, but subjects it withal to his own purposes and moulds it according to his own peculiarities. The throng and succession of ideas, thoughts, feelings, imaginations, aspirations, which pass within him, the abstractions, the juxtapositions, the comparisons, the discrimination, the conceptions, which are so original in him, his views of external things, his judgments upon life, manners, and history, the exercises of his art, of his humour, of his depth, of his sagacity—all these innumerable and incessant creations, the very pulsation and throbbing of his intellect, does he image forth, to all does he give utterance, in a corresponding language, which is as multiform as this inward mental action itself and analogous to it, the faithful expression of his intense personality, attending on his own inward world of thought as its very shadow; so that we might as well say that one man's shadow is another's as that the style of a really gifted mind can belong to any but himself. It follows him about as a shadow. His thought and feeling are personal, and so his language is personal. (*I. of U.*, p. 276)

It is the fire within the author's breast which overflows in the torrent of his burning, irresistible eloquence; it is the poetry of his inner soul which relieves itself in the Ode or the Elegy; and his mental attitude and bearing, the beauty of his moral countenance, the force and keenness of his logic, are imaged in the tenderness or energy or richness of his language. Nay, according to the well-known line, "facit indignatio *versus*": not the words alone, but even the rhythm, the metre, the verse, will be the contemporaneous offspring of the emotion or imagination which possesses him. (*I. of U.*, p. 279)

Instances and patterns, not logical reasonings, are the living conclusions which alone have a hold over the affections, or can form the character. (*D. and A.*, p. 297)

THAT pomp of language, that full and tuneful diction, that felicitousness in the choice and exquisiteness in the collocation of words, which to prosaic writers seem artificial, is nothing else but the mere habit and way of a lofty intellect. Aristotle, in his sketch of the magnanimous man, tells us that his voice is deep, his motions slow, and his stature commanding. In like manner, the elocution of a great intellect is great. His language expresses, not only his great thoughts, but his great self. Certainly he might use fewer words than he uses; but he fertilizes his simplest ideas, and germinates into a multitude of details, and prolongs the march of his sentences, and sweeps round to the full diapason of his harmony, as if κύδεϊ γαίων, rejoicing in his own vigour and richness of resource. I say, a narrow critic will call it verbiage, when really it is a sort of fulness of heart, parallel to that which makes the merry boy whistle as he walks, or the strong man, like the smith in the novel, flourish his club when there is no one to fight with. Shakespeare furnishes us with frequent instances of this peculiarity, and all so beautiful, that it is difficult to select for quotation. (*I. of U.*, p. 280)

A GREAT author is not one who merely has a *copia verborum*, whether in prose or verse, and can, as it were, turn on at his will any number of splendid phrases and swelling sentences; but he is one who has something to say and knows how to say it. I do not claim for him, as such, any great depth of thought, or breadth of view, or philosophy, or sagacity, or knowledge of human nature, or experience of human life, though these additional gifts he may have, and the more he has of them the greater he is; but I ascribe to him, as his characteristic gift, in a large sense the faculty of expression.

He is master of the two-fold "logos"—the thought and the word, distinct but inseparable from each other. He may, if so be, elaborate his compositions, or he may pour out his improvisations, but in either case he has but one aim, which he keeps steadily before him and is conscientious and single-minded in fulfilling. That aim is to give forth what he has within him; and from his very earnestness it comes to pass that, whatever be the splendour of his diction or the harmony of his periods, he has with him the charm of an incommunicable simplicity. Whatever be his subject, high or low, he treats it suitably and for its own sake. (*I. of U.*, p. 291f.)

HE WRITES passionately, because he feels keenly; forcibly, because he conceives vividly; he sees too clearly to be vague; he is too serious to be otiose; he can analyse his subject, and therefore he is rich; he embraces it as a whole and in its parts, and therefore he is consistent; he has a firm hold of it, and therefore he is luminous. When his imagination wells up, it overflows in ornament; when his heart is touched, it thrills along his verse. He always has the right word for the right idea, and never a word too much. If he is brief, it is because few words suffice; when he is lavish of them, still each word has its mark, and aids, not embarrasses, the vigorous march of his elocution. He expresses what all feel, but all cannot say, and his sayings pass into proverbs among his people, and his phrases become household words and idioms of their daily speech, which is tessellated with the rich fragments of his language—as we see in foreign lands the marbles of Roman grandeur worked into the walls and pavements of modern palaces. (*I. of U.*, p. 292f.)

LET us consider how differently young and old are affected by the words of some classic author, such as Homer or Horace. Passages which to a boy are but rhetorical commonplaces, neither better nor worse than a hundred others which any clever writer might supply, which he gets by heart and thinks very fine, and imitates, as he thinks, successfully, in his own flowing versification, at length come home to him, when long years have passed and he has had experience of life, and pierce him, as if he had never before known them, with their sad earnestness and vivid exactness. Then he comes to understand how it is that lines—the birth of some chance morning or evening at an Ionian festival or among the Sabine hills —have lasted generation after generation, for thousands of years, with a power over the mind and a charm which the current literature of his own day, with all its obvious advantages, is utterly unable to rival. Perhaps this is the reason of the medieval opinion about Virgil as if a prophet or magician: his single words and phrases, his pathetic half-lines, giving utterance, as the voice of Nature herself, to that pain and weariness, yet hope of better things, which is the experience of her children in every time. (*G. of A.*, p. 78f.)

READING, as we do, the Gospels from our youth up, we are in danger of becoming so familiar with them as to be dead to their force, and to view them as mere history. (*G. of A.*, p. 79)

MR. KINGSLEY begins [his charge] by exclaiming,—"O the chicanery, the wholesale fraud, the vile hypocrisy, the conscience-killing tyranny of Rome! We have not far to seek for an evidence of it! There's Father Newman to wit: one living specimen is worth a hundred dead ones. He, a Priest, writing of Priests, tells us that lying is never any harm."

I interpose: "You are taking a most extraordinary liberty with my name. If I have said this, tell me when and where."

Mr. Kingsley replies: "You said it, Reverend Sir, in a sermon which you preached, when a Protestant, as Vicar of St. Mary's, and published in 1844; and I could read you a very salutary lecture on the effects which that Sermon had at the time on my own opinion of you."

I make answer: "Oh. . . *Not*, it seems, as a priest speaking of priests; but let us have the passage."

Mr. Kingsley relaxes: "Do you know I like your *tone*. From your *tone*, I rejoice, greatly rejoice, to be able to believe that you did not mean what you said."

I rejoin: "*Mean* it! I maintain I never *said* it, whether as a Protestant or as a Catholic."

Mr. Kingsley replies: "I waive that point."

I object: "Is it possible? What? waive the main question! I either said it or I didn't. You have made a monstrous charge against me; direct, distinct, public. You are bound to prove it as directly, as distinctly, as publicly;—or to own you can't!"

"Well," says Mr. Kingsley, "if you are quite sure you did not say it, I'll take your word for it; I really will."

My *word!* I am dumb. Somehow I thought that it was my *word* that happened to be on trial. The *word* of a Professor of lying, that he does not lie!

But Mr. Kingsley reassures me: "We are both gentlemen," he says: "I have done as much as one English gentleman can expect from another."

I begin to see: he thought me a gentleman at the very time that he said I taught lying on system. After all, it is not I, but it is Mr. Kingsley who did not mean what he said. "Habemus confitentem reum." So we have confessedly come round to this, preaching without practising; the common theme of satirists from Juvenal to Walter Scott! (*Apol.*, p. 20f.)

I CANNOT be sorry to have forced my Accuser [Mr. Kingsley] to bring out in fulness his charges against me. It is far better that he should discharge his thoughts upon me in my lifetime, than after I am dead. Under the circumstances I am happy in having the opportunity of reading the worst that can be said of me by a writer who has taken pains with his work and is well satisfied with it. I account it a gain to be surveyed from without by one who hates the principles which are nearest to my heart, has no personal knowledge of me to set right his misconceptions of my doctrine, and who has some motive or other to be as severe with me as he can possibly be.

I am sitting at home without a thought of Mr. Kingsley; he wantonly breaks in upon me with the charge that I had *"informed"* the world "that Truth for its own sake *need not* and on the whole *ought not to be* a virtue with the Roman clergy." When challenged on the point he cannot bring a fragment of evidence in proof of his assertion, and he is convicted of false witness by the voice of the world. Well, I should have thought that he had now nothing whatever more to do. "Vain man!" he seems to make answer, "what simplicity in you to think so! If you have not broken one commandment, let us see whether we cannot convict you of the breach of another. If you are not a swindler or forger, you are guilty of arson or burglary. By hook or by crook you shall not escape. Are *you* to suffer or *I?* What does it matter to you who are going off the stage, to receive a slight additional daub upon a character so deeply stained already? But think of me, the immaculate lover of Truth, so observant of '*hault courage* and strict honour,'—and (*aside*)—'and not as this publican'—do you think I can let you go scot free instead of myself? No; *noblesse oblige.* Go to the shades, old man, and boast that Achilles sent you thither."

But I really feel sad for what I am obliged now to say. I am in warfare with him, but I wish him no ill;—it is very difficult to get up resentment towards persons whom one has never seen. It is easy enough to be irritated with friends or foes *vis-à-vis;* but, though I am writing with all my heart against what he has said of me, I am not conscious of personal unkindness towards himself. I think it necessary to write as I am writing, for my own sake, and for the sake of the Catholic Priesthood; but I wish to impute nothing worse to him than that he has been furiously carried away by his feelings. Yet what shall I say of the upshot of all his talk of my economies and equivocations and the like? What is the precise *work* which it is directed to effect? I am at war with him; but there is such a thing as legitimate warfare: war has its laws: there are things which may fairly be done, and things which may not be done. I say it with shame and with stern sorrow;—he has attempted a great transgression; he has attempted to poison by anticipation the public mind against me, John Henry Newman, and to infuse into the imaginations of my readers, suspicion and mistrust of everything that I may say in reply to him. This I call *poisoning the wells.*

I can hardly get myself to protest against a method of controversy so base and cruel, lest in doing so, I should be violating my self-respect and self-possession; but most base and most cruel it is. We all know how our imagination runs away with us, how suddenly and at what a pace;—the saying, "Cæsar's wife should not be suspected," is an instance of what I mean. The habitual prejudice, the humour of the moment, is the turning-point which leads us to read a defence in a good sense or a bad. We interpret it by our antecedent impressions. The very same sentiments, according as our jealousy is or is not awake, or our aversion stimulated, are tokens of truth or of dissimulation and pretence.

Controversies should be decided by the reason; is it legitimate warfare to appeal to the misgivings of the public mind and to its dislikings? Anyhow, if my Accuser is able thus to practise upon my readers, the more I succeed, the less will be my success. If I am natural, he will tell them "Ars est celare artem;" if I am convincing, he will suggest that I am an able logician; if I show warmth, I am acting the indignant innocent; if I am calm, I am thereby detected as a smooth hypocrite; if I clear up difficulties, I am too plausible and perfect to be true. The more triumphant are my statements, the more certain will be my defeat.

So will it be if my Accuser succeeds in his manœuvre; but I do not for an instant believe that he will. Whatever judgment my readers may eventually form of me from these pages, I am confident that they will believe me in what I shall say in the course of them. I have no misgiving at all, that they will be ungenerous or harsh towards a man who has been so long before the eyes of the world;

who has so many to speak of him from personal knowledge; whose natural impulse it has ever been to speak out; who has ever spoken too much rather than too little; who would have saved himself many a scrape, if he had been wise enough to hold his tongue; who has ever been fair to the doctrines and arguments of his opponents; who has never slurred over facts and reasonings which told against himself; who has never given his name or authority to proofs which he thought unsound, or to testimony which he did not think at least plausible; who has never shrunk from confessing a fault when he felt that he had committed one; who has ever consulted for others more than for himself; who has given up much that he loved and prized and could have retained, but that he loved honesty better than name, and Truth better than dear friends.

For twenty years and more I have borne an imputation, of which I am at least as sensitive, who am the object of it, as they can be, who are only the judges. I have not set myself to remove it, first, because I never have had an opening to speak, and, next, because I never saw in them the disposition to hear. I am bound now as a duty to myself, to the Catholic cause, to the Catholic Priesthood, to give account of myself without any delay, when I am so rudely and circumstantially charged with Untruthfulness. I accept the challenge; I shall do my best to meet it, and I shall be content when I have done so. (*Apol.,* p. 69ff.)

[MR. KINGSLEY] asks what I *mean;* not about my words, not about my arguments, not about my actions, as his ultimate point, but about that living intelligence, by which I write, and argue, and act. He asks about my Mind and its Beliefs and its sentiments; and he shall be answered;—not for his own sake, but for mine, for the sake of the Religion which I profess, and of the Priesthood in which I am unworthily included, and of my friends and of my foes, and of that general public which consists of neither one nor the other, but of well-wishers, lovers of fair play, sceptical cross-questioners, interested inquirers, curious lookers-on, and simple strangers unconcerned yet not careless about the issue,—for the sake of all these he shall be answered.

My perplexity had not lasted half an hour. I recognized what I had to do, though I shrank from both the task and the exposure which it would entail. I must, I said, give the true key to my whole life; I must show what I am, that it may be seen what I am not, and that the phantom may be extinguished which gibbers instead of me. I wish to be known as a living man, and not as a scarecrow which is dressed up in my clothes. False ideas may be refuted indeed by arguments, but by true ideas alone are they expelled.

I will vanquish, not my Accuser, but my judges. I will indeed answer his charges and criticisms on me one by one, lest any one should say that they are unanswerable, but such a work shall not be the scope nor the substance of my reply. I will draw out, as far as may be, the history of my mind; I will state the point at which I began, in what external suggestion or accident each opinion had its rise, how far and how they developed from within, how they grew, were modified, were combined, were in collision with each other, and were changed; again how I conducted myself towards them, and how, and how far, and for how long a time, I thought I could hold them consistently with the ecclesiastical engagements which I had made and with the position which I held.

I must show,—what is the very truth,—that the doctrines which I held, and have held for so many years, have been taught me (speaking humanly) partly by the suggestion of Protestant friends, partly by the teaching of books, and partly by the action of my own mind: and thus I shall account for that phenomenon which to so many seems so wonderful, that I should have left "my kindred and my father's house" for a Church from which once I turned away with dread; so wonderful to them! as if forsooth a Religion which has flourished through so many ages, among so many nations, amid such varieties of social life, in such contrary classes and conditions of men, and after so many revolutions, political and civil, could not subdue the reason and overcome the heart, without the aid of fraud in the process and the sophistries of the schools. (*Apol.*, p. 99ff.)

I HAVE closed this history of myself [the *Apologia*] with St. Philip's name upon St. Philip's feast-day; and, having done so, to whom can I more suitably offer it, as a memorial of affection and gratitude, than to St. Philip's sons, my dearest brothers of this House, the Priests of the Birmingham Oratory, AMBROSE ST. JOHN, HENRY AUSTIN MILLS, HENRY BITTLESTON, EDWARD CASWALL, WILLIAM PAINE NEVILLE, and HENRY IGNATIUS DUDLEY RYDER? who have been so faithful to me; who have been so sensitive of my needs; who have been so indulgent to my failings; who have carried me through so many trials; who have grudged no sacrifice, if I asked for it; who have been so cheerful under discouragements of my causing; who have done so many good works, and let me have the credit of them;—with whom I have lived so long, with whom I hope to die.

And to you especially, dear AMBROSE ST. JOHN; whom

God gave me, when He took every one else away; who are the link between my old life and my new; who have now for twenty-one years been so devoted to me, so patient, so zealous, so tender; who have let me lean so hard upon you; who have watched me so narrowly; who have never thought of yourself, if I was in question.

And in you I gather up and bear in memory those familiar affectionate companions and counsellors, who in Oxford were given to me, one after another, to be my daily solace and relief; and all those others, of great name and high example, who were my thorough friends, and showed me true attachment in times long past; and also those many younger men, whether I knew them or not, who have never been disloyal to me by word or deed; and of all these, thus various in their relations to me, those more especially who have since joined the Catholic Church.

And I earnestly pray for this whole company, with a hope against hope, that all of us, who once were so united, and so happy in our union, may even now be brought at length, by the Power of the Divine Will, into One Fold and under One Shepherd. (*Apol.*, p. 371f.)

IS THE enemy of Christ, and His Church, to arise out of a certain special falling away from GOD? And is there no reason to fear that some such Apostasy is gradually preparing, gathering, hastening on in this very day? For is there not at this very time a special effort made almost all over the world, that is, every here and there, more or less in sight or out of sight, in this or that place, but most visibly or formidably in its most civilized and powerful parts, an effort to do without Religion? Is there not an opinion avowed and growing, that a nation has nothing to do with Religion; that it is merely a matter for each man's own conscience?—which is all one with saying that we may let the Truth fail from the earth without trying to continue it in and on after our time. Is there not a vigorous and united movement in all countries to cast down the Church of Christ from power and place?

Is there not a feverish and ever-busy endeavour to get rid of the necessity of Religion in public transactions? for example, an attempt to get rid of oaths, under a pretence that they are too sacred for affairs of common life, instead of providing that they be taken more reverently and more suitably? an attempt to educate without Religion?—that is, by putting all forms of Religion together, which comes to the same thing;—an attempt to enforce temperance, and the virtues which flow from it, without Religion, by means of Societies which are built on mere principles of utility? an attempt to make *expedience,* and not *truth,* the end and the rule of measures of State and the enactments of Law? an attempt to make numbers, and not the Truth, the ground of maintaining, or not maintaining, this or that creed, as if we had any reason whatever in Scripture for thinking that the many will be in the right, and the few in the wrong? an attempt to deprive the Bible of its one meaning to the exclusion of all other, to make people think that it may have an hundred meanings all equally good, or, in other words, that it has no meaning at all, is a dead letter, and may be put aside? an attempt to supersede Religion altogether, as far as it is external or objective, as far as it is displayed in ordinances, or can be expressed by written words,—to confine it to our inward feelings, and thus, considering how variable, how evanescent our feelings are, an attempt, in fact, to destroy Religion?

Surely, there is at this day a confederacy of evil, marshalling its hosts from all parts of the world, organizing itself, taking its measures, enclosing the Church of Christ as in a net, and preparing the way for a general Apostasy from it. This Apostasy, and all its tokens and instruments, are of the Evil One, and savour of death. Far be it from any of us to be of those simple ones who are taken in that snare which is circling around us! Far be it from us to be seduced with the fair promises in which Satan is sure to hide his poison! Do you think he is so unskilful in his craft, as to ask you openly and plainly to join him in his warfare against the Truth? No; he offers you baits to tempt you. He promises you civil liberty; he promises you equality; he promises you trade and wealth; he promises you a remission of taxes; he promises you reform; he tempts you to rail against your rulers and superiors; he does so himself, and induces you to imitate him; or he promises you illumination,—he offers you knowledge, science, philosophy, enlargement of mind. He scoffs at times gone by; he scoffs at every institution which reveres them. He prompts you what to say, and then listens to you, and praises you, and encourages you. He bids you mount aloft. He shows you how to become as gods. Then he laughs and jokes with you, and gets intimate with you; he takes your hand, and gets his fingers between yours, and grasps them, and then you are his. (*D. and A.*, p. 59ff.)

WE must make up our minds to be ignorant of much, if we would know anything. And we must make our choice between risking Science, and risking Religion. (*D. and A.*, p. 280)

IN MORALS, as in physics, the stream cannot rise higher than its source. Christianity raises men from earth, for it comes from heaven; but human morality creeps, struts, or frets upon the earth's level, without wings to rise. The Knowledge School does not contemplate raising man above himself; it merely aims at disposing of his existing powers and tastes, as is most convenient, or is practicable under circumstances. It finds him, like the victims of the French Tyrant, doubled up in a cage in which he can neither lie, stand, sit, nor kneel, and its highest desire is to find an attitude in which his unrest may be least. Or it finds him like some musical instrument, of great power and compass, but imperfect; from its very structure some keys must ever be out of tune, and its object, when ambition is highest, is to throw the *fault* of its nature where least it will be observed. It leaves man where it found him—man, and not an Angel—a sinner, not a Saint. (*D. and A.*, p. 272f.)

o MY brethren, O kind and affectionate hearts, O loving friends, should you know any one whose lot it has been, by writing or by word of mouth, in some degree to help you thus to act; if he has ever told you what you knew about yourselves, or what you did not know; has read to you your wants or feelings, and comforted you by the very reading; has made you feel that there was a higher life than this daily one, and a brighter world than that you see; or encouraged you, or sobered you, or opened a way to the inquiring, or soothed the perplexed; if what he has said or done has ever made you take interest in him, and feel well inclined towards him; remember such a one in time to come, though you hear him not, and pray for him, that in all things he may know God's will, and at all times he may be ready to fulfil it. (*S. S. D.*, p. 409)*

ST. PAUL says in one place that his Apostolical power is given him to edification, and not to destruction. There can be no better account of the Infallibility of the Church. It is a supply for a need, and it does not go beyond that need. Its object is, and its effect also, not to enfeeble the freedom or vigour of human thought in religious speculation, but to resist and control its extravagance. (*Apol.*, p. 344)

FROM the time that I became a Catholic, of course I have no further history of my religious opinions to narrate. In saying this, I do not mean to say that my mind has been idle, or that I have given up thinking on theological subjects; but that I have had no changes to record, and have had no anxiety of heart whatever. I have been in perfect peace and contentment. I never have had one doubt. I was not conscious to myself, on my conversion, of any difference of thought or of temper from what I had before. I was not conscious of firmer faith in the fundamental truths of revelation, or of more self-command; I had not more fervour; but it was like coming into port after a rough sea; and my happiness on that score remains to this day without interruption. (*Apol.*, p. 331)

THE Romans deified Law, as the Athenians deified the Beautiful. (*H. S.* III. 81)

* From Newman's last Anglican sermon.

THE love of the Beautiful will not conquer the world, but, like the voice of Orpheus, it may for a while carry it away captive. (*H. S.*, III. 83)

IN THIS world no one rules by mere love; if you are but amiable, you are no hero; to be powerful, you must be strong, and to have dominion you must have a genius for organizing. (*H. S.* III. 85)

THE safeguard of Faith is a right state of heart. (*O. U. S.*, p. 234)

CALCULATION never made a hero. (*D. Ch. D.*, p. 328)

THE primary duty of a literary man is to have clear conceptions, and to be exact and intelligible in expressing them. (*G. of A.*, p. 20f.)

A MAN *is* responsible for his faith, because he is responsible for his likings and dislikings, his hopes and his opinions, on all of which his faith depends. (*O. U. S.*, p. 192)

HALF the controversies in the world are verbal ones; and could they be brought to a plain issue, they would be brought to a prompt termination. When men understand each other's meaning, they see, for the most part, that controversy is either superfluous or hopeless. (*O. U. S.*, p. 200f.)

ST. PHILIP NERI lived in [the sixteenth century] an age as traitorous to the interests of Catholicism as any that preceded it, or can follow it. He lived at a time when pride mounted high, and the senses held rule; a time when kings and nobles never had more of state and homage, and never less of personal responsibility and peril; when mediæval winter was receding, and the summer sun of civilization was bringing into leaf and flower a thousand forms of luxurious enjoyment; when a new world of thought and beauty had opened upon the human mind, in the discovery of the treasures of classic literature and art.

He saw the great and the gifted, dazzled by the Enchantress, and drinking in the magic of her song; he saw the high and the wise, the student and the artist, painting, and poetry, and sculpture, and music, and architecture, drawn within her range, and circling round the abyss: he saw heathen forms mounting thence, and forming in the thick air:—all this he saw, and he perceived that the mischief was to be met, not with argument, not with science, not with protests and warnings, not by the recluse or the preacher, but by means of the great counter fascination of purity and truth. [It was his aim] to yield to the stream, and direct the current, which he could not stop, of science, literature, art, and fashion, and to sweeten and to sanctify what God had made very good and man had spoilt.

He came to the Eternal City and he sat himself down there, and his home and his family gradually grew up around him, by the spontaneous accession of materials from without. He did not so much seek his own as draw them to him. He sat in his small room, and they in their gay worldly dresses, the rich and the wellborn, as well as the simple and the illiterate, crowded into it. In the mid-heats of summer, in the frosts of winter, still was he in that low and narrow cell at San Girolamo, reading the hearts of those who came to him, and curing their souls' maladies by the very touch of his hand. It was a vision of the Magi worshipping the infant Saviour, so pure and innocent, so sweet and beautiful was he; and so loyal and so dear to the gracious Virgin Mother. And they who came remained gazing and listening, till at length, first one and then another threw off their bravery, and took his poor cassock and girdle instead: or, if they kept it, it was to put haircloth under it, or to take on them a rule of life, while to the world they looked as before. (*I. of U.*, p. 234ff.)

POETRY is a method of relieving the over-burdened mind; it is a channel through which emotion finds expression, and that a safe, regulated expression. Now what is the Catholic Church, viewed in her human aspect, but a discipline of the affections and passions? What are her ordinances and practices but the regulated expression of keen, or deep, or turbid feeling, and thus a "cleansing," as Aristotle would word it, of the sick soul?

She is the poet of her children; full of music to soothe the sad and control the wayward,—wonderful in story for the imagination of the romantic; rich in symbol and imagery, so that gentle and delicate feelings, which will not bear words, may in silence intimate their presence or commune with themselves. Her very being is poetry; every psalm, every petition, every collect, every versicle, the cross, the mitre, the thurible, is a fulfilment of some dream of childhood or aspiration of youth. Such poets as are born under her shadow, she takes into her service; she sets them to write hymns, or to compose

chants, or to embellish shrines, or to determine ceremonies, or to marshal processions; nay, she can even
make schoolmen of them, as she made St. Thomas, till
logic becomes poetical. (*E. C. and H.* II. 442f.)

THOUGH the sea was their element, [the Northmen]
were equally prepared to avail themselves of the land,
and equally at home upon it. They seemed to have a
ubiquitous presence. As the lightning, the hurricane, or
the plague sweeps through its inevitable circuit, or hur-
ries along its capricious zigzag path, so these marauders
were at one time lurking in the deep creek and darting
out upon the unsuspecting voyager, at another hurrying
along the coast, making their sudden descent and as suddenly re-embarking; and at another, landing, leaving
their vessels, and running up the country. They had come
and gone and done their terrible work, before they could
be encountered. Now they were on the German Sea, now
in the Bay of Biscay, now in the Mediterranean. They
were at Rouen, at Amiens, at Paris, on the Loire, in
Burgundy. They were in Brittany, in Aquitaine, at Bor-
deaux. They landed on the coast near Cadiz, and faced
the Moorish monarch in three battles. Then, again, they
were in Holland, on Walcheren, at Cambray, at Hainault,
at Louvain, and other parts of Belgium. They set fire
to the villages and to the crops; they massacred the
peasantry; they crucified, they impaled; they spitted in-
fants on their lances; cruelty was one of the glories of
their warfare. (*H. S.* III. 269)

LATITUDINARIANS, while they profess charity towards all
doctrines, nevertheless count it heresy to oppose the principle of latitude. (*O. U. S.*, p. 296)

THOUGH of the same stock as the Saxons, the Northmen were gifted with a more heroic cast of soul. Perhaps it was the peculiar scenery and climate of their native homes which suggested to them such lofty aspirations, and such enthusiastic love of danger and hardship. The stillness of the desert may fill the fierce Arab with a rapturous enjoyment, and the interminable forests of Britain or Germany might breathe profound mystery; but the icy mountains and the hoarse resounding waves of the North nurtured warriors of a princely stature, both in mind and body, befitting the future occupants of European thrones. Cradled in the surge and storm, they were spared the temptation of indolence and luxury; they neither worshipped the vivifying powers of nature with the Greek, nor with the Sabean did they kiss the hand to the bright stars of heaven; but, while they gave a personal presence and volition to the fearful or the beautiful spirits which haunted the mountains or lay in ambush in the mist, they understood by daily experience that good could not be had by the mere wishing, and they made it a first article in their creed that their reward was future, and that their present must be toil. (*H. S.* III. 290)

YOU may hold the most fatal errors or the most insane extravagances, if you hold them in a misty confused way. Numbers will persist in countenancing and defending even these. But ask yourself what you mean by your words, try to master your own thoughts, try to ascertain what you believe and what you do not, avoid big professions, blundering epithets and languid generalities; and lookers-on at once begin to wonder why you should so needlessly hurt people's feelings and damage your own cause. In the present day mistiness is the mother of wisdom. (*E. C. and H.*, p. 301f.)

IT IS the least pardonable fault in an orator to fail in clearness of style, and the most pardonable fault of a poet. (*G. of A.*, p. 21)

THOSE political institutions are the best which subtract as little as possible from a people's natural independence as the price of their protection. The stronger you make the Ruler, the more he can do for you, *but* the more he also can do against you; the weaker you make him, the less he can do against you, *but* the less also he can do for you. Put a sword into the Ruler's hands, it is at his option to use or not use it against you; reclaim it, and who is to use it for you? Thus, if States are free, they are feeble; if they are vigorous, they are high-handed. I am not speaking of a nation or a people, but of a State as such; and I say, the more a State secures to itself of rule and centralization, the more it can do for its subjects externally; and the more it grants to them of liberty and self-government, the less it can do against them internally: and thus a despotic government is the best for war, and a popular government the best for peace. (*D. and A.*, p. 325f.)

[THE typical Englishman] is indeed rough, surly, a bully and a bigot; these are his weak points: but if ever there was a generous, good, tender heart, it beats within his breast. Most placable, he forgives and forgets: forgets, not only the wrongs he has received, but the insults he has inflicted. Such he is commonly; for doubtless there are times and circumstances in his dealings with foreigners in which, whether when in despair or from pride, he becomes truculent and simply hateful; but at home his bark is worse than his bite. He has qualities, excellent for the purposes of neighbourhood and intercourse; and he has, besides, a shrewd sense, and a sobriety of judgment, and a practical logic, which passion does not cloud, and which makes him understand that good-fellowship is not only commendable, but expedient too. And he has within him a spring of energy, pertinacity, and perseverance, which makes him as busy and effective in a colony as he is companionable at home. Some races do not move at all; others are ever jostling against each other; the Englishman is ever stirring, yet never treads too hard upon his fellow-countryman's toes. He does his work neatly, silently, in his own place; he looks to himself, and can take care of himself; and he has that instinctive veneration for the law, that he can worship it even in the abstract, and thus is fitted to go shares with others all around him in that political sovereignty, which other races are obliged to concentrate in one ruler. (*D. and A.*, p. 334f.)

SOME races are like children, and require a despot to nurse, and feed, and dress them, to give them pocket money, and take them out for airings. Others, more manly, prefer to be rid of the trouble of their affairs, and use their Ruler as their mere manager and man of business. (*D. and A.*, p. 336)

WHO can know himself, and the multitude of subtle influences which act upon him? (*Apol.*, p. 191)

AS DESPOTISMS keep their subjects in ignorance, lest they should rebel, so will a free people maim and cripple their government, lest it should tyrannize.

This is human nature; the more powerful a man is, the more jealous is he of other powers. Little men endure little men; but great men aim at a solitary grandeur. (*D. and A.*, p. 342)

ENGLAND, surely, is the paradise of little men, and the purgatory of great ones. (*D. and A.*, p. 343)

WHEN Mr. Gladstone asks Catholics how they can obey the Queen and yet obey the Pope, since it may happen that the commands of the two authorities may clash, I answer, that it is my *rule*, both to obey the one and to obey the other, but that there is no rule in this world without exceptions, and if either the Pope or the Queen demanded of me an "Absolute Obedience," he or she would be transgressing the laws of human nature and human society. I give an absolute obedience to neither. Further, if ever this double allegiance pulled me in contrary ways, which in this age of the world I think it never will, then I should decide according to the particular case, which is beyond all rule, and must be decided on its own merits. I should look to see what theologians could do for me, what the Bishops and clergy around me, what my confessor; what friends whom I revered: and if, after all, I could not take their view of the matter, then I must rule myself by my own judgment and my own conscience. (*A. D.* II. 243f.)

WHAT a number of beautiful and wonderful objects does nature present on every side of us! And how little we know concerning them! Why do rivers flow? Why does rain fall? Why does the sun warm us? And the wind, why does it blow? Here our natural reason is at fault; we know, I say, that it is the spirit in man and beast that makes man and beast move, but reason tells us of no spirit abiding in what is commonly called the natural world, to make it perform its ordinary duties. Of course it is God's will which sustains it; all this wonderful harmony is the work of Angels. Those events which we ascribe to chance, as the weather, or to nature, as the seasons, are duties done to that God Who maketh His Angels to be winds and His Ministers a flame of fire. (*P. and P. S.* II. 359f.)

A LITERATURE, when it is formed, is a national and historical fact; it is a matter of the past and the present, and can be as little ignored as the present, as little undone as the past. Every great people has a character of its own, which it manifests and perpetuates in a variety of ways. It develops into a monarchy or republic;—by means of commerce or in war, in agriculture or in manufactures, or in all of these at once; in its cities, its public edifices and works, bridges, canals, and harbours; in its laws, traditions, customs, and manners; in its songs and its proverbs; in its religion; in its line of policy, its bearing, its action towards foreign nations; in its alliances, fortunes, and the whole course of its history. (*I. of U.*, p. 308f.)

IN truth, every event of this world is a type of those that follow, history proceeding forward as a circle ever enlarging. (*D. and A.*, p. 49)

FIRST-RATE excellence in literature, as in other matters, is either an accident or the outcome of a process; and in either case demands a course of years to secure. We cannot reckon on a Plato, we cannot force an Aristotle, any more than we can command a fine harvest, or create a coal-field.

If a literature be the voice of a particular nation, it requires a territory and a period, as large as that nation's extent and history, to mature in. It is broader and deeper than the capacity of any body of men, however gifted, or any system of teaching, however true. It is the exponent, not of truth, but of nature, which is true only in its elements. It is the result of the mutual action of a hundred simultaneous influences and operations, and the issue of a hundred strange accidents in independent places and times; it is the scanty compensating produce of the wild discipline of the world and of life, so fruitful in failures; and it is the concentration of those rare manifestations of intellectual power, which no one can account for. It is made up, in the particular language here under consideration, of human beings as heterogeneous as Burns and Bunyan, De Foe and Johnson, Goldsmith and Cowper, Law and Fielding, Scott and Byron. (*I. of U.*, p. 311)

CERTAIN masters of composition, as Shakespeare, Milton, and Pope, the writers of the Protestant Bible and Prayer Book, Hooker and Addison, Swift, Hume, and Goldsmith, have been the making of the English language; and as that language is a fact, so is the literature a fact, by which it is formed, and in which it lives. Men of great ability have taken it in hand, each in his own day, and have done for it what the master of a gymnasium does for the bodily frame. They have formed its limbs, and developed its strength; they have endowed it with vigour, exercised it in suppleness and dexterity, and taught it grace. They have made it rich, harmonious, various, and precise. They have furnished it with a variety of styles, which from their individuality may almost be called dialects, and are monuments both of the powers of the language and the genius of its cultivators. (*I. of U.*, p. 312f.)

LIKE music, [style] has seized upon the public mind; and the literature of England is no longer a mere letter, printed in books, and shut up in libraries, but it is a living voice, which has gone forth in its expressions and its sentiments into the world of men, which daily thrills upon our ears and syllables our thoughts, which speaks to us through our correspondents, and dictates when we put pen to paper. (*I. of U.*, p. 313)

ONE literature may be better than another, but bad will be the best, when weighed in the balance of truth and morality. It cannot be otherwise; human nature is in all ages and all countries the same; and its literature, therefore, will ever and everywhere be one and the same also. Man's work will savour of man; in his elements and powers excellent and admirable, but prone to disorder and excess, to error and to sin. Such too will be his literature; it will have the beauty and the fierceness, the sweetness and the rankness, of the natural man, and, with all its richness and greatness, will necessarily offend the senses of those who, in the Apostle's words, are really "exercised to discern between good and evil." "It is said of the holy Sturme," says an Oxford writer, "that, in passing a horde of unconverted Germans, as they were bathing and gambolling in the stream, he was so over-powered by the intolerable scent which arose from them that he nearly fainted away." National Literature is, in a parallel way, the untutored movements of the reason, imagination, passions, and affections of the natural man, the leapings and the friskings, the plungings and the snortings, the sportings and the buffoonings, the clumsy play and the aimless toil, of the noble, lawless savage of God's intellectual creation. (*I. of U.*, p. 316f.)

ABSOLUTE proof can never be furnished to us by the logic of words, for as certitude is of the mind, so is the act of inference which leads to it. Every one who reasons is his own centre. (*G. of A.*, p. 345)

YOU must either conquer the world or the world will conquer you. You must be either master or slave. (*S. S. D.*, p. 111)

IT IS to the living mind that we must look for the means of using correctly principles of whatever kind. (*G. of A.*, p. 360)

WHATEVER passages may be gleaned from [Shake-speare's] dramas disrespectful to ecclesiastical authority, still these are but passages; on the other hand, there is in Shakespeare neither contempt of religion nor scepti-cism, and he upholds the broad laws of moral and divine truth with the consistency and severity of an Æschylus, Sophocles, or Pindar. There is no mistaking in his works on which side lies the right; Satan is not made a hero, nor Cain a victim, but pride is pride, and vice is vice, and, whatever indulgence he may allow himself in light thoughts or unseemly words, yet his admiration is reserved for sanctity and truth. From the second chief fault of Literature he is not so free; but, often as he may offend against modesty, he is clear of a worse charge, sensuality, and hardly a passage can be instanced in all that he has written to seduce the imagination or to excite the passions. (*I. of U.,* p. 318)

WHAT the world is, such it has ever been; we know the contempt which the educated pagans had for the martyrs and confessors of the Church; and it is shared by the anti-Catholic bodies of this day. (*I. of U.,* p. 206)

THE oracles of Divine Truth, as time goes on, do but repeat the one message from above which they have ever uttered, since the tongues of fire attested the coming of the Paraclete; still, as time goes on, they utter it with greater force and precision, under diverse forms, with fuller luminousness, and a richer ministration of thought, statement, and argument. They meet the varying wants, and encounter the special resistance of each successive age; and, though prescient of coming errors and their remedy long before, they cautiously reserve their new enunciation of the old Truth, till it is imperatively demanded. And, as it happens in kings' cabinets, that surmises arise, and rumors spread, of what is said in council, and is in course of preparation, and secrets perhaps get wind, true in substance or in direction, though distorted in detail; so too, before the Church speaks, one or other of her forward children speaks for her, and, while he does anticipate to a certain point what she is about to say or enjoin, he states it incorrectly, makes it error instead of truth, and risks his own faith in the process. Indeed, this is actually one source, or rather concomitant, of heresy, the presence of some misshapen, huge, and grotesque foreshadow of true statements which are to come. (*H. S.* III. 192f.)

THE swarm [of locusts] grew and grew till it became a compact body, as much as a furlong square; yet it was but the vanguard of a series of similar hosts, formed one after another out of the hot mould or sand, rising into the air like clouds, enlarging into a dusky canopy, and then discharged against the fruitful plain. At length the huge innumerous mass was put into motion, and began its career, darkening the face of day. Thus they advanced, host after host, for a time wafted on the air, and gradually declining to the earth, while fresh broods were carried over the first, and neared the earth, after a longer flight, in their turn. For twelve miles did they extend from front to rear, and their whizzing and hissing could be heard for six miles on every side of them. The bright sun, though hidden by them, illumined their bodies, and was reflected from their quivering wings; and as they heavily fell earthward they seemed like the innumerable flakes of a yellow-coloured snow. And like snow did they descend, a living carpet, or rather pall, upon fields, crops, gardens, copses, groves, orchards, vineyards, olive-woods, orangeries, palm plantations, and the deep forests, sparing nothing within their reach, and, where there was nothing to devour, lying helpless in drifts, or crawling forward obstinately, as they best might, with the hope of prey.

Their masses filled the bottoms of the ravines and hollow ways, impeding the traveller as he rode forward on his journey, and trampled by thousands under his horse-hoofs. In vain was all this overthrow and waste by the roadside; in vain their loss in river, pool, and water-course. The poor peasants hastily dug pits and trenches as their enemy came on; in vain they filled them from the wells or with lighted stubble. Heavily and thickly did the locusts fall; they were lavish of their lives; they choked the flame and the water, which destroyed them the while, and the vast living hostile armament still moved on.

They moved right on like soldiers in their ranks, stopping at nothing, and straggling for nothing; they carried a broad furrow or wheal all across the country, black and loathsome, while it was as green and smiling on each side of them and in front as it had been before they came. Before them, in the language of prophets, was a paradise, and behind them a desert. They are daunted by nothing; they surmount walls and hedges, and enter enclosed gardens or inhabited houses.

They come up to the walls of Sicca, and are flung against them into the ditch. Not a moment's hesitation or delay; they recover their footing, they climb up the wood or stucco, they surmount the parapet, or they have entered in at the windows, filling the apartments, and the most private and luxurious chambers, not one or two, like stragglers at forage or rioters after a victory, but in order of battle, and with the array of an army. Choice plants or flowers about the *impluvia* and *xysti*, for ornament or refreshment, myrtles, oranges, pomegranates, the rose and the carnation, have disappeared. They dim the bright marbles of the walls and the gilding of the ceilings. They enter the triclinium in the midst of the banquet; they crawl over the viands and spoil what they do not devour. Unrelaxed by success and by enjoyment, onward they go; a secret mysterious instinct keeps them together, as if they had a king over them. They move along the floor in so strange an order that they seem to be a tessellated pavement themselves, and to be the artificial embellishment of the place; so true are their lines, and so perfect is the pattern they describe. Onward they go, to the market, to the temple sacrifices, to the baker's stores, to the cookshops, to the confectioners, to the druggists; nothing comes amiss to them; wherever man has aught to eat or drink, there are they, reckless of death, strong of appetite, certain of conquest. (*Cal.*, p. 170ff.)

[IN GETHSEMANE] in that most awful hour, knelt the Saviour of the world, putting off the defences of His divinity, dismissing His reluctant Angels, who in myriads were ready at His call, and opening His arms, baring His breast, sinless as He was, to the assault of His foe,— of a foe whose breath was a pestilence, and whose embrace was an agony. There He knelt, motionless and still, while the vile and horrible fiend clad His spirit in a robe steeped in all that is hateful and heinous in human crime, which clung close round His heart, and filled His conscience, and found its way into every sense and pore of His mind, and spread over Him a moral leprosy, till He almost felt Himself to be that which He never could be, and which His foe would fain have made Him.

Oh, the horror, when He looked, and did not know

Himself, and felt as a foul and loathsome sinner, from His vivid perception of that mass of corruption which poured over His head and ran down even to the skirts of His garments! Oh, the distraction, when He found His eyes, and hands, and feet, and lips, and heart, as if the members of the Evil One, and not of God! Are these the hands of the Immaculate Lamb of God, once innocent, but now red with ten thousand barbarous deeds of blood? Are these His lips, not uttering prayer, and praise, and holy blessings, but as if defiled with oaths, and blasphemies, and doctrines of devils? or His eyes, profaned as they are by all the evil visions and idolatrous fascinations for which men have abandoned their adorable Creator? And His ears, they ring with sounds of revelry and of strife; and His heart is frozen with avarice, and cruelty, and unbelief; and His very memory is laden with every sin which has been committed since the fall, in all regions of the earth.

Who does not know the misery of a haunting thought which comes again and again, in spite of rejection, to annoy, if it cannot seduce? or of some odious and sickening imagination, in no sense one's own, but forced upon the mind from without? or of evil knowledge, gained with or without a man's fault, but which he would give a great price to be rid of at once and for ever? And adversaries such as these gather around Thee, Blessed Lord, in millions now; they come in troops more numerous than the locust or the palmer-worm, or the plagues of hail, and flies, and frogs, which were sent against Pharaoh. Of the living and of the dead and of the as yet unborn, of the lost and of the saved, of Thy people and of strangers, of sinners and of saints, all sins are there.

It is the long history of a world, and God alone can

bear the load of it. Hopes blighted, vows broken, lights quenched, warnings scorned, opportunities lost; the innocent betrayed, the young hardened, the penitent relapsing, the just overcome, the aged failing; the sophistry of misbelief, the wilfulness of passion, the obduracy of pride, the tyranny of habit, the canker of remorse, the wasting fever of care, the anguish of shame, the pining of disappointment, the sickness of despair; such cruel, such pitiable spectacles, such heartrending, revolting, detestable, maddening scenes; nay, the haggard faces, the convulsed lips, the flushed cheek, the dark brow of the willing slaves of evil, they are all before Him now; they are upon Him and in Him. They are with Him instead of that ineffable peace which has inhabited His soul since the moment of His conception. They are upon Him, they are all but His own; He cries to His Father as if He were the criminal, not the victim; His agony takes the form of guilt and compunction. He is doing penance, He is making confession, He is exercising contrition, with a reality and a virtue infinitely greater than that of all saints and penitents together; for He is the One Victim for us all, the sole Satisfaction, the real Penitent, all but the real sinner.

He rises languidly from the earth, and turns around to meet the traitor and his band, now quickly nearing the deep shade. He turns, and lo! there is blood upon His garment and in His footprints. Whence come these first-fruits of the passion of the Lamb? no soldier's scourge has touched His shoulders, nor the hangman's nails His hands and feet. He has bled before His time; He has shed blood; yes, and it is His agonising soul which has broken up His framework of flesh and poured it forth. His passion has begun from within. That tormented Heart, the seat of tenderness and love, began at length to labour and to beat with vehemence beyond its nature; "the foundations of the great deep were broken up;" the red streams rushed forth so copious and fierce as to overflow the veins, and bursting through the pores, they stood in a thick dew over His whole skin; then forming into drops, they rolled down full and heavy, and drenched the ground.

"My soul is sorrowful even unto death," He said. (*D. M. C.*, p. 336ff.)

THE flame of love will not be bright unless the substance which feeds it be pure and unadulterate; and the most dazzling purity is but as iciness and desolation unless it draws its life from fervent love. (*D. M. C.*, p. 63)

ALL aberrations are founded on, and have their life in, some truth or other. (*Apol.*, p. 281)

IT WAS a formal banquet, given by a rich Pharisee, to honour, yet to try, our Lord. Magdalen came, young and beautiful, and "rejoicing in her youth," "walking in the ways of her heart and the gaze of her eyes:" she came as if to honour that feast, as women were wont to honour such festive doings, with her sweet odours and cool unguents for the forehead and hair of the guests. And he, the proud Pharisee, suffered her to come, so that she touched not him; let her come as we might suffer inferior animals to enter our apartments, without caring for them; perhaps suffered her as a necessary embellishment of the entertainment, yet as having no soul, or as destined to perdition, but anyhow as nothing to him. He, proud being, and his brethren like him, might "compass sea and land to make one proselyte;" but, as to looking into that proselyte's heart, pitying its sin, and trying to heal it, this did not enter into the circuit of his thoughts. No, he thought only of the necessities of his banquet, and he let her come to do her part, such as it was, careless what her life was, so that she did that part well, and confined herself to it.

But, lo, a wondrous sight! was it a sudden inspiration, or a mature resolve? was it an act of the moment, or the result of a long conflict?—but behold, that poor, many-coloured child of guilt approaches to crown with her sweet ointment the head of Him to whom the feast was given; and see, she has stayed her hand. She has looked, and she discerns the Immaculate, the Virgin's Son, "the brightness of the Eternal Light, and the spotless mirror of God's majesty." She looks, and she recognizes the Ancient of Days, the Lord of life and death, her Judge; and again she looks, and she sees in His face and in His mien a beauty, and a sweetness, awful, serene, majestic, more than that of the sons of men, which paled all the splendour of that festive room.

Again she looks, timidly yet eagerly, and she discerns in His eye, and in His smile, the loving-kindness, the tenderness, the compassion, the mercy of the Saviour of man. She looks at herself, and oh! how vile, how hideous is she, who but now was so vain of her attractions!—how withered is that comeliness, of which the praises ran through the mouths of her admirers!—how loathsome has become the breath, which hitherto she thought so fragrant, savouring only of those seven bad spirits which dwell within her! And there she would have stayed, there she would have sunk on the earth, wrapped in her confusion and in her despair, had she not cast one glance again on that all-loving, all-forgiving Countenance. He is looking at her: it is the Shepherd looking at the lost sheep, and the lost sheep surrenders herself to Him. He speaks not, but He eyes her; and she draws nearer to Him.

She draws near, seeing nothing but Him, and caring neither for the scorn of the proud, nor the jests of the profligate. She draws near, not knowing whether she shall be saved or not, not knowing whether she shall be received, or what will become of her; this only knowing that He is the Fount of holiness and truth, as of mercy, and to whom should she go, but to Him who hath the words of eternal life? "Destruction is thine own, O Israel; in Me only is thy help. Return unto Me, and I will not turn away My face from thee: for I am holy, and will not be angry for ever." "Behold we come unto thee; for Thou art the Lord our God. Truly the hills are false, and the multitude of the mountains: Truly the Lord our God is the salvation of Israel."

Wonderful meeting between what was most base and what is most pure! Those wanton hands, those polluted lips, have touched, have kissed the feet of the Eternal, and He shrank not from the homage. And as she hung over them, and as she moistened them from her full eyes, how did her love for One so great, yet so gentle, wax vehement within her, lighting up a flame which never was to die from that moment even for ever! and what excess did it reach, when He recorded before all men her forgiveness, and the cause of it! "Many sins are forgiven her, for she loved much; but to whom less is forgiven, the same loveth less. And He said unto her, Thy sins are forgiven thee; thy faith hath made thee safe, go in peace." (*D. M. C.*, p. 75ff.)

THE natural conscience of man, if cultivated from within, if enlightened by those external aids which in varying degrees are given him in every place and time, would teach him much of his duty to God and man, and would lead him on, by the guidance both of Providence and grace, into the fulness of religious knowledge; but, generally speaking, he is contented that it should tell him very little, and he makes no efforts to gain any juster views than he has at first, of his relations to the world around him and to his Creator. (*S. V. O.*, p. 20f.)

[THE Pharisee] looked upon himself with great complacency, for the very reason that the standard was so low, and the range so narrow, which he assigned to his duties towards God and man. He used, or misused, the traditions in which he had been brought up, to the purpose of persuading himself that perfection lay in merely answering the demands of society. He professed, indeed, to pay thanks to God, but he hardly apprehended the existence of any direct duties on his part towards his Maker. He thought he did all that God required, if he satisfied public opinion. To be religious, in the Pharisee's sense, was to keep the peace towards others, to take his share in the burdens of the poor, to abstain from gross vice, and to set a good example. His alms and fastings were not done in penance, but because the world asked for them; penance would have implied the consciousness of sin; whereas it was only Publicans, and such as they, who had anything to be forgiven. And these indeed were the outcasts of society, and despicable; but no account lay against men of well-regulated minds such as his: men who were well-behaved, decorous, consistent, and respectable. He thanked God he was a Pharisee, and not a penitent. (*S. V. O.*, p. 21f.)

VIRTUE, according to Xenophon, consists mainly in command of the appetites and passions, and in serving others in order that they may serve us. He says, in the well-known Fable, called The Choice of Hercules, that Vice has no real enjoyment even of those pleasures which it aims at; that it eats before it is hungry, and drinks before it is thirsty, and slumbers before it is wearied. It never hears, he says, that sweetest of voices, its own praise; it never sees that greatest luxury among sights, its own good deeds. It enfeebles the bodily frame of the young, and the intellect of the old.

Virtue, on the other hand, rewards young men with the praise of their elders, and it rewards the aged with the reverence of youth; it supplies them pleasant memories and present peace; it secures the favour of heaven, the love of friends, a country's thanks, and, when death comes, an everlasting renown. In all such descriptions, virtue is something external; it is not concerned with motives or intentions; it is occupied in deeds which bear upon society, and which gain the praise of men; it has little to do with conscience and the Lord of conscience; and knows nothing of shame, humiliation, and penance. It is in substance the Pharisee's religion, though it be more graceful and more interesting.

Now this age is as removed in distance, as in character, from that of the Greek philosopher; yet who will say that the religion which it acts upon is very different from the religion of the heathen? (*S. V. O.*, p. 23f.)

THE religion of the natural man is often very beautiful on the surface, but worthless in God's sight; good, as far as it goes, but worthless and hopeless, because it does not go further, because it is based on self-sufficiency, and results in self-satisfaction. I grant, it may be beautiful to look at, as in the instance of the young ruler whom our Lord looked at and loved, yet sent away sad; it may have all the delicacy, the amiableness, the tenderness, the religious sentiment, the kindness, which is actually seen in many a father of a family, many a mother, many a daughter, in the length and breadth of these kingdoms, in a refined and polished age like this; but still it is rejected by the heart-searching God, because all such persons walk by their own light, not by the True Light of men, because self is their supreme teacher, and because they pace round and round in the small circle of their own thoughts and of their own judgments, careless to know what God says to them, and fearless of being condemned by Him, if only they stand approved in their own sight. (*S. V. O.*, p. 25f.)

[THE progress of the individual] is a living growth, not a mechanism; and its instruments are mental acts, not the formulas and contrivances of language. (*G. of A.*, p. 350)

GREAT things are done by devotion to one idea; there is one class of geniuses, who would never be what they are, could they grasp a second. The calm philosophical mind, which contemplates parts without denying the whole, and the whole without confusing the parts, is notoriously indisposed to action; whereas single and simple views arrest the mind, and hurry it on to carry them out. (*H. S.* III. 197)

THERE is just one Name in the whole world that lives; it is the Name of One who passed His years in obscurity, and who died a malefactor's death. Eighteen hundred years have gone by since that time, but still It has Its hold upon the human mind. It has possessed the world, and It maintains possession. Amid the most various nations, under the most diversified circumstances, in the most cultivated, in the rudest races and intellects, in all classes of society, the Owner of that great Name reigns. High and low, rich and poor, acknowledge Him. Millions of souls are conversing with Him, are venturing at His word, are looking for His presence. Palaces sumptuous, innumerable, are raised to His honour; His image, in its deepest humiliations, is triumphantly displayed in the proud city, in the open country, at the corners of streets, on the tops of mountains. It sanctifies the ancestral hall, the closet, and the bedchamber; it is the subject for the exercise of the highest genius in the imitative arts. It is worn next the heart in life; it is held before the failing eyes in death. Here, then, is One Who is not a mere name; He is no empty fiction; He is a substance; He is dead and gone, but still He lives—as the living, energetic thought of successive generations, and as the awful motive power of a thousand great events. (*S. V. O.*, p. 44f.)

IN A time when colleges were unknown, and the young scholar was commonly thrown upon the dubious hospitality of a great city, Abelard might even be thought careful of his honour, that he went to lodge with an

old ecclesiastic, had not his host's niece Eloisa lived
with him. A more subtle snare was laid for him than
beset the heroic champion or the all-accomplished monarch of Israel; for sensuality came upon him under the
guise of intellect, and it was the high mental endowments of Eloisa, who became his pupil, speaking in her
eyes, and thrilling on her tongue, which were the intoxication and the delirium of Abelard. (*H. S.* III. 200f.)

THERE are those, and of the highest order of sanctity
too, as far as our eyes can see, in whom the supernatural
combines with nature, instead of superseding it,—invigo-
rating it, elevating it, ennobling it; and who are not
the less men, because they are saints. They do not put
away their natural endowments, but use them to the
glory of the Giver; they do not act beside them, but
through them; they do not eclipse them by the brightness
of Divine grace, but only transfigure them. They are
versed in human knowledge; they are busy in human
society; they understand the human heart; they can
throw themselves into the minds of other men; and all
this in consequence of natural gifts and secular education. While they themselves stand secure in the blessedness of purity and peace, they can follow in imagination
the ten thousand aberrations of pride, passion, and remorse.

The world is to them a book, to which they are drawn
for its own sake, which they read fluently, which interests them naturally,—though, by reason of the grace
which dwells within them, they study it and hold
converse with it for the glory of God and the salvation
of souls. Thus they have the thoughts, feelings, frames
of mind, attractions, sympathies, antipathies of other

men, so far as these are not sinful, only they have these properties of human nature purified, sanctified, and exalted; and they are only made more eloquent, more poetical, more profound, more intellectual, by reason of their being more holy. In this latter class I may perhaps without presumption place many of the early Fathers, St. Chrysostom, St. Gregory Nazianzen, St. Athanasius, and above all, the great Saint of this day, St. Paul the Apostle. (*S. V. O.*, p. 92f.)

IN ALL of the separate actions of the intellect, the individual is supreme and responsible to himself, nay, under circumstances, may be justified in opposing himself to the judgment of the whole world; though he uses rules to his great advantage, as far as they go, and is in consequence bound to use them. (*G. of A.*, p. 353)

[ARE] those few scattered worshippers, *the* Roman Catholics [of England], to form a Church! Shall the past be rolled back? Shall the grave open? Shall the Saxons live again to God? Shall the shepherds, watching their poor flocks by night, be visited by a multitude of the heavenly army and hear how their Lord has been new-born in their own city? Yes; for grace can, where nature cannot. The world grows old, but the Church is ever young. She can, in any time, at her Lord's will, "inherit the Gentiles and inhabit the desolate cities." "Arise, Jerusalem, for thy light is come, and the glory of the Lord is risen upon thee. Behold, darkness shall cover the earth, and a mist the people; but the Lord shall arise upon thee and His glory shall be seen upon thee. Lift up thine eyes round about and see; all these are gathered together, they come to thee; thy sons shall come from afar, and thy daughters shall rise up at thy side." "Arise, make haste, my love, my dove, my beautiful one, and come. For the winter is now past and the rain is over and gone. The flowers have appeared in our land . . . the fig-tree hath put forth her green figs; the vines in flower yield their sweet smell. Arise, my love, my beautiful one, and come."

It is the time for thy visitation. Arise, Mary, and go forth in thy strength into that north country, which once was thine own, and take possession of a land which knows thee not! Arise, Mother of God, and with thy thrilling voice, speak to those who labour with child, and are in pain, till the babe of grace leaps within them! Shine on us, dear Lady, with thy bright countenance, like the sun in his strength, *O stella matutina*, O harbinger of peace, till our year is one perpetual May! From thy sweet eyes, from thy pure smile, from thy majestic brow, let ten thousand influences rain down, not to confound or overwhelm, but to persuade, to win over thine enemies! O Mary, my hope, O Mother undefiled, fulfil to us the promise of this Spring!

A second temple rises on the ruins of the old. Canterbury has gone its way, and York is gone, and Durham is gone, and Winchester is gone. It was sore to part with them. We clung to the vision of past greatness, and would not believe it could come to naught; but the Church in England has died, and the Church lives again. Westminster and Nottingham, Beverley and Hexham, Northampton and Shrewsbury, if the world lasts, shall be names as musical to the ear, as stirring to the heart, as the glories we have lost; and saints shall arise out of them, if God so will, and doctors once again shall give the law to Israel, and preachers call to penance and to justice, as at the beginning. (*S. V. O.*, p. 176ff.)

IT IS not God's way that great blessings should descend without the sacrifice first of great sufferings. If the truth is to be spread to any wide extent among this people, how can we dream, how can we hope, that trial and trouble shall not accompany its going forth? And we have already, if it may be said without presumption, to commence our work withal, a large store of merits. We have no slight outfit for our opening warfare. Can we religiously suppose that the blood of our martyrs, three centuries ago and since, shall never receive its recompense? Those priests, secular and regular, did they suffer for no end? or rather, for an end which is not yet accomplished?

The long imprisonment, the fetid dungeon, the weary suspense, the tyrannous trial, the barbarous sentence, the savage execution, the rack, the gibbet, the knife, the caldron, the numberless tortures of those holy victims, O my God, are they to have no reward? Are Thy martyrs to cry from under Thine altar for their loving vengeance on this guilty people, and to cry in vain? Shall they lose life, and not gain a better life for the children of those who persecuted them? Is this Thy way, O my God, righteous and true? Is it according to Thy promise, O King of Saints, if I may dare talk to Thee of justice? Didst not Thou Thyself pray for Thine enemies upon the Cross, and convert them? Did not Thy first martyr win Thy great Apostle, then a persecutor, by his loving prayer? And in that day of trial and desolation for England, when hearts were pierced through and through with Mary's woe, at the crucifixion of Thy body mystical, was not every tear that flowed, and every drop of blood that was shed, the seeds of a future harvest when they who sowed in sorrow were to reap in joy?

And as that suffering of the martyrs is not yet recompensed, so, perchance, it is not yet exhausted. Something, for what we know, remains to be undergone to complete the necessary sacrifice. May God forbid it, for this poor nation's sake! But still, could we be surprised, my Fathers and my Brothers, if the winter even now should not yet be quite over? Have we any right to take it strange, if, in this English land, the spring-time of the Church should turn out to be an English spring—an uncertain, anxious time of hope and fear, of joy and suffering—of bright promise and budding hopes, yet withal of keen blasts and cold showers and sudden storms? One thing alone I know, that according to our need so will be our strength. (*S. V. O.*, p. 178ff.)

THE regions on which [the North] has principally expended its fury are those whose fatal beauty, or richness of soil, or perfection of cultivation, or exquisiteness of produce, or amenity of climate, makes them objects of desire to the barbarian.

These regions have neither the inducement nor the means to retaliate upon their ferocious invaders. The relative position of the combatants must always be the same while the combat lasts. The South has nothing to win, the North nothing to lose; the North nothing to offer, the South nothing to covet. Nor is this all: the North, as in an impregnable fortress, defies the attack of the South. Immense trackless solitudes; no cities, no tillage, no roads; deserts, forests, marshes; bleak table-lands, snowy mountains; unlocated, flitting, receding populations; no capitals, or marts, or strong places, or fruitful vales, to hold as hostages for submission; fearful winters and many months of them;—nature herself fights and conquers for the barbarian.

What madness shall tempt the South to undergo extreme risks without the prospect or chance of a return? True it is, ambition, whose very life is a fever, has now and then ventured on the reckless expedition; but from the first page of history to the last, from Cyrus to Napoleon, what has the Northern war done for the greatest warriors but destroy the flower of their armies and the *prestige* of their name? Our maps, in placing the North at the top, and the South at the bottom of the sheet, impress us, by what may seem a sophistical analogy, with the imagination that Huns or Moguls, Kalmucks or Cossacks, have been a superincumbent mass, descending by a sort of gravitation upon the fair territories which lie below them. Yet this is substantially true;— though the attraction towards the South is of a moral, not of a physical nature, yet an attraction there is, and a huge conglomeration of destructive elements hangs over us, and from time to time rushes down with an awful irresistible momentum. Barbarism is ever impending over the civilized world. (*H. S.* i. 11f.)

I CONFESS to a delight in reading the lives, and dwelling on the characters and actions, of the Saints of the first ages, such as I receive from none besides them; and for this reason, because we know so much more about them than about most of the Saints who come after them. People are variously constituted; what influences one does not influence another. There are persons of warm imaginations, who can easily picture to themselves what they never saw. They can at will see Angels and Saints hovering over them when they are in church; they see their lineaments, their features, their motions, their gestures, their smile or their grief. They can go home and draw what they have seen, from the vivid memory of what, while it lasted, was so transporting.

I am not one of such; I am touched by my five senses, by what my eyes behold and my ears hear. I am touched by what I read about, not by what I myself create. As faith need not lead to practice, so in me mere imagination does not lead to devotion. I gain more from the life of our Lord in the Gospels than from a treatise *de Deo*. I gain more from three verses of St. John than from the three points of a meditation. I like a Spanish crucifix of painted wood more than one from Italy, which is made of gold. I am more touched by the Seven Dolors than by the Immaculate Conception; I am more devout to St. Gabriel than to one of Isaiah's seraphim.

I do not say that my way is better than another's; but it is my way, and an allowable way. And it is the reason why I am so specially attached to the Saints of the third and fourth century, because we know so much about them. This is why I feel a devout affection for St. Chrysostom. He and the rest of them have written autobiography on a large scale; they have given us their own histories, their thoughts, words, and actions, in a number of goodly folios, productions which are in themselves some of their meritorious works.

The Ancient Saints have left behind them just that kind of literature which more than any other represents the abundance of the heart, which more than any other approaches to conversation; I mean correspondence. Why is it that we feel an interest in Cicero which we cannot feel in Demosthenes or Plato? Plato is the very type of

soaring philosophy, and Demosthenes of forcible eloquence; Cicero is something more than an orator and a
sage; he is not a mere ideality, he is a man and a brother;
he is one of ourselves. We do not merely believe it, or
infer it, but we have the enduring and living evidence
of it—how? In his letters.

When I read St. Augustine or St. Basil, I hold converse with a beautiful grace-illumined soul, looking out
into this world of sense, and leavening it with itself;
when I read a professed life of him, I am wandering
in a labyrinth of which I cannot find the centre and
heart, and am but conducted out of doors again when
I do my best to penetrate within. (*H. S.* II. 217ff.)

A BRIGHT, cheerful, gentle soul; a sensitive heart, a temperament open to emotion and impulse; and all this elevated, refined, transformed by the touch of heaven,—
such was St. John Chrysostom; winning followers, rivet-
ing affections, by his sweetness, frankness, and neglect of
self. In his labours, in his preaching, he thought of others
only. He was, indeed, a man to make both friends and
enemies; to inspire affection and to kindle resentment;
but his friends loved him with a love "stronger" than
"death," and more burning than "hell"; and it was well
to be so hated, if he was so beloved.

Here he differs, as far as I can judge, from his brother
saints and doctors of the Greek Church, St. Basil and St.
Gregory Nazianzen. They were scholars, shy perhaps and
reserved; and though they had not given up the secular
state, they were essentially monks. There is no evidence,
that I remember, to show that they attached men to
their persons. They, as well as John, had a multitude of
enemies; and were regarded, the one with dislike, the

other perhaps with contempt; but they had not, on the other hand, warm, eager, sympathetic, indignant, agonized friends. There is another characteristic in Chrysostom, which perhaps gained for him this great blessing. He had, as it would seem, a vigour, elasticity, and, what may be called, sunniness of mind, all his own. He was ever sanguine, seldom sad. Basil had a life-long malady, involving continual gnawing pain and a weight of physical dejection. He bore his burden well and gracefully, like the great Saint he was, as Job bore his; but it was a burden like Job's.

He was a calm, mild, grave, autumnal day; St. John Chrysostom was a day in springtime, bright and rainy, and glittering through its rain. Gregory was the full summer, with a long spell of pleasant stillness, its monotony relieved by thunder and lightning. And St. Athanasius figures to us the stern persecuting winter, with its wild winds, its dreary wastes, its sleep of the great mother, and the bright stars shining overhead. He and Chrysostom have no points in common; but Gregory was a dethroned Archbishop of Constantinople, like Chrysostom, and, again, dethroned by his brethren the Bishops.

Like Basil, too, Chrysostom was bowed with infirmities of body; he was often ill; he was thin and wizened; cold was a misery to him; heat affected his head; he scarcely dared touch wine; he was obliged to use the bath; obliged to take exercise, or rather to be continually on the move. Whether from a nervous or febrile complexion, he was warm in temper; or at least, at certain times, his emotion struggled hard with his reason. But he had that noble spirit which complains as little as possible; which makes the best of things; which soon recovers its equanimity, and hopes on in circumstances when others sink down in despair. (*H. S.* II. 234ff.)

[ST. CHRYSOSTOM'S] charm lies, as I have said, in his habit and his power of throwing himself into the minds of others, of imagining with exactness and with sympathy circumstances or scenes which were not before him, and of bringing out what he has apprehended in words as direct and vivid as the apprehension. His page is like the table of a *camera lucida*, which represents to us the living action and interaction of all that goes on around us. That loving scrutiny, with which he follows the Apostles as they reveal themselves to us in their writings, he practices in various ways towards all men, living and dead, high and low, those whom he admires and those whom he weeps over. He writes as one who was ever looking out with sharp but kind eyes upon the world of men and their history; and hence he has always something to produce about them, new or old, to the purpose of his argument, whether from books or from the experience of life. Head and heart were full to overflowing with a stream of mingled "wine and milk," of rich vigorous thought and affectionate feeling. (*H. S.* II. 289)

AS WELL can there be filial love without the fact of a father, as devotion without the fact of a Supreme Being. (*Apol.*, p. 150)

THE Euxine! that strange mysterious sea, which typifies the abyss of outer darkness, as the blue Mediterranean basks under the smile of heaven in the centre of civilization and religion. The awful, yet splendid drama of man's history has mainly been carried on upon the

Mediterranean shores; while the Black Sea has ever been on the very outskirts of the habitable world, and the scene of wild unnatural portents; with legends of Prometheus on the savage Caucasus, of Medea gathering witch herbs in the moist meadows of the Phasis, and of Iphigenia sacrificing the shipwrecked stranger in Taurica; and then again, with the more historical, yet not more grateful visions of barbarous tribes, Goths, Huns, Scythians, Tartars, flitting over the steppes and wastes which encircle its inhospitable waters. To be driven [as was Chrysostom] from the bright cities and sunny clime of Italy or Greece to such a region, was worse than death. (*H. S.* ii. 233)

WHAT is so ordinary and familiar to us as the elements, what so simple and level to us as their presence and operation? yet how their character changes, and how they overmaster us, and triumph over us, when they come upon us in their fullness! The invisible air, how gentle is it, and intimately ours! we breathe it momentarily, nor could we live without it; it fans our cheek, and flows around us, and we move through it without effort, while it obediently recedes at every step we take, and obsequiously pursues us as we go forward. Yet let it come in its power, and that same silent fluid, which was just now the servant of our necessity or caprice, takes us up on its wings with the invisible power of an Angel, and carries us forth into the regions of space, and flings us down headlong upon the earth. Or go to the spring, and draw thence at your pleasure, for your cup or your pitcher, in supply of your wants; you have a ready servant, a domestic ever at hand, in large quantity or in small, to satisfy your thirst, or to purify you from the dust and mire of the world.

Go from home, reach the coast; and you will see that same humble element transformed before your eyes. You were equal to it in its condescension, but who shall gaze without astonishment at its vast expanse in the bosom of the ocean? who shall hear without awe the dashing of its mighty billows along the beach? who shall without terror feel it heaving under him, and swelling and mounting up, and yawning wide, till he, its very sport and mockery, is thrown to and fro, hither and thither, at the mere mercy of a power which was just now his companion and almost his slave? Or, again, approach the flame: it warms you, and it enlightens you; yet approach not too near, presume not, or it will change its nature. That very element which is so beautiful to look at, so brilliant in its character, so graceful in its figure, so soft and lambent in its motion, will be found in its essence to be of a keen, resistless nature; it tortures, it consumes, it reduces to ashes that of which it was just before the illumination and the life.

So it is with the attributes of God; our knowledge of them serves us for our daily welfare; they give us light and warmth and food and guidance and succor; but go forth with Moses upon the mount and let the Lord pass by, or with Elias stand in the desert amid the wind, the earthquake, and the fire, and all is mystery and darkness; all is but a whirling of the reason, and a dazzling of the imagination, and an overwhelming of the feelings, reminding us that we are but mortal men and He is God, and that the outlines which nature draws for us are not His perfect image, nor to be pronounced inconsistent with those further lights and depths with which it is invested by Revelation. (*D. M. C.*, p. 318ff.)

I SEE One dropping blood, gashed by the thong, and stretched upon the Cross, and He is God. It is no tale of human woe from the Cross. He seems to say,—I cannot move, though I am omnipotent, for sin has bound Me here. I had had it in mind to come on earth among innocent creatures, more fair and lovely than them all, with a face more radiant than the Seraphim, and a form as royal as that of Archangels, to be their equal yet their God, to fill them with My grace, to receive their worship, to enjoy their company, and to prepare them for the heaven to which I destined them; but, before I carried My purpose into effect, they sinned, and lost their inheritance; and so I come indeed, but come, not in that brightness in which I went forth to create the morning stars and to fill the sons of God with melody, but in deformity and in shame, in sighs and tears, with blood upon My cheek, and with My limbs laid bare and rent. Gaze on Me, O My children, if you will, for I am helpless; gaze on your Maker, whether in contempt, or in faith and love. Here I wait, upon the Cross, the appointed time, the time of grace and mercy; here I wait till the end of the world, silent and motionless, for the conversion of the sinful and the consolation of the just; here I remain in weakness and shame, though I am so great in heaven, till the end, patiently expecting My full catalogue of souls, who, when time is at length over, shall be the reward of My passion and the triumph of My grace to all eternity. (*D. M. C.*, p. 321f.)

THE earth is full of the marvels of Divine power; "Day to day uttereth speech, and night to night showeth knowledge." The tokens of Omnipotence are all around us, in the world of matter, and the world of man; in the dis-

pensation of nature, and in the dispensation of grace. To
do impossibilities, I may say, is the prerogative of Him
who made all things out of nothing, who foresees all
events before they occur, and controls all wills without
compelling them. In emblem of this His glorious attribute, He came to His disciples in the passage I have
read to you, walking upon the sea,—the emblem or hiero-
glyphic among the ancients of the impossible, to show
them that what is impossible with man is possible with
God. He who could walk the waters, could also ride triumphantly upon what is still more fickle, unstable, tumultuous, treacherous—the billows of human wills, human purposes, human hearts. (*S. V. O.*, p. 121f.)

THE men commonly held in popular estimation are
greatest at a distance; they become small as they are
approached. (*O. U. S.*, p. 95)

WE HAVE familiar experience of the order, the con-
stancy, the perpetual renovation of the material world
which surrounds us. Frail and transitory as is every
part of it, restless and migratory as are its elements, never
ceasing as are its changes, still it abides. It is bound together by a law of permanence, it is set up in unity; and,
though it is ever dying, it is ever coming to life again.
Dissolution does but give birth to fresh modes of organization, and one death is the parent of a thousand lives.
Each hour, as it comes, is but a testimony, how fleeting,
yet how secure, how certain, is the great whole. It is like
an image on the waters, which is ever the same, though
the waters ever flow. Change upon change—yet one
change cries out to another, like the alternate Seraphim,

in praise and in glory of their Maker. The sun sinks to rise again; the day is swallowed up in the gloom of the night, to be born out of it, as fresh as if it had never been quenched. Spring passes into summer, and through summer and autumn into winter, only the more surely, by its own ultimate return, to triumph over that grave, towards which it resolutely hastened from its first hour. We mourn over the blossoms of May, because they are to wither; but we know, withal, that May is one day to have its revenge upon November, by the revolution of that solemn circle which never stops—which teaches us in our height of hope, ever to be sober, and in our depth of desolation, never to despair. (*S. V. O.*, p. 163f.)

THE mind ranges to and fro, and spreads out and advances forward with a quickness which has become a proverb, and a subtlety and versatility which baffle investigation. It passes on from point to point, gaining one by some indication; another on a probability; then availing itself of an association; then falling back on some received law; next seizing on testimony; then committing itself to some popular impression, or some inward instinct, or some obscure memory; and thus it makes progress not unlike a clamberer on a steep cliff, who, by quick eye, prompt hand, and firm foot, ascends, how he knows not himself, by personal endowments and by practice, rather than by rule, leaving no track behind him, and unable to teach another. It is not too much to say that the stepping by which great geniuses scale the mountain of truth is as unsafe and precarious to men in general as the ascent of a skilful mountaineer up a literal crag. It is a way which they alone can take; and its justification lies alone in their success. And such mainly is the way in which all men, gifted or not gifted, commonly reason—not by rule, but by an inward faculty. Reasoning, then, or the exercise of reason, is a living, spontaneous energy within us, not an art. (*O. U. S.*, p. 257)

TIME was when the forefathers of our race were a savage tribe, inhabiting a wild district beyond the limits of this quarter of the earth. Whatever brought them thither, they had no local attachments there or political settlement; they were a restless people, and whether urged forward by enemies or by desire of plunder, they left their place, and passing through the defiles of the mountains on the frontiers of Asia, they invaded Europe, setting out on a journey towards the farther west. Generation after generation passed away; and still this fierce and haughty race moved forward. On, on they went; but travel availed them not; the change of place could bring them no truth, or peace, or hope, or stability of heart; they could not flee from themselves.

They carried with them their superstitions and their sins, their gods of iron and of clay, their savage sacrifices, their lawless witchcrafts, their hatred of their kind, and their ignorance of their destiny. At length they buried themselves in the deep forests of Germany, and gave themselves up to indolent repose; but they had not found their rest; they were still heathens, making the fair trees, the primeval work of God, and the innocent beasts of the chase, the objects and the instruments of their idolatrous worship. And, last of all, they crossed over the strait and made themselves masters of this island, and gave their very name to it; so that, whereas it had hitherto been called Britain, the southern part, which

was their main seat, obtained the name of England.
(*S. V. O.*, p. 124f.)

SUDDENLY the word of truth came to our ancestors in
this island and subdued them to its gentle rule; the grace
of God fell on them, and, without compulsion, as the
historian tells us, the multitude became Christian; when
all was tempestuous, and hopeless, and dark, Christ like
a vision of glory came walking to them on the waves of
the sea. Then suddenly there was a great calm; a change
came over the pagan people in that quarter of the country where the gospel was first preached to them; and
from thence the blessed influence went forth, it was
poured out over the whole land, till one and all, the
Anglo-Saxon people, were converted by it.

In a hundred years the work was done; the idols, the
sacrifices, the mummeries of paganism flitted away and
were not, and the pure doctrine and heavenly worship
of the Cross were found in their stead. The fair form
of Christianity rose up and grew and expanded like a
beautiful pageant from north to south; it was majestic,
it was solemn, it was bright, it was beautiful and pleasant, it was soothing to the griefs, it was indulgent to
the hopes of man; it was at once a teaching and a worship; it had a dogma, a mystery, a ritual of its own; it
had an hierarchical form.

A brotherhood of holy pastors, with miter and crosier
and uplifted hand, walked forth and blessed and ruled
a joyful people. The crucifix headed the procession, and
simple monks were there with hearts in prayer, and sweet
chants resounded, and the holy Latin tongue was heard,
and boys came forth in white, swinging censers, and the
fragrant cloud arose, and mass was sung, and the Saints

were invoked; and day after day, and in the still night, and over the woody hills and in the quiet plains, as constantly as sun and moon and stars go forth in heaven, so regular and solemn was the stately march of blessed services on earth, high festival, and gorgeous procession, and soothing dirge, and passing bell, and the familiar evening call to prayer; till he who recollected the old pagan time, would think it all unreal that he beheld and heard, and would conclude he did but see a vision, so marvelously was heaven let down upon earth, so triumphantly were chased away the fiends of darkness to their prison below. (*S. V. O.,* p. 127f.)

WHATEVER be the risk of corruption from intercourse with the world around, such a risk must be encountered if a great idea is duly to be understood, and much more if it is to be fully exhibited. It is elicited and expanded by trial, and battles into perfection and supremacy. Nor does it escape the collision of opinion even in its earlier years, nor does it remain truer to itself, and with a better claim to be considered one and the same, though externally protected from vicissitude and change. It is indeed sometimes said that the stream is clearest near the spring. Whatever use may fairly be made of this image, it does not apply to the history of a philosophy or belief, which on the contrary is more equable, and purer, and stronger, when its bed has become deep, and broad, and full. It necessarily rises out of an existing state of things, and for a time savors of the soil. Its vital element needs disengaging from what is foreign and temporary, and is employed in efforts after freedom which become more vigorous and hopeful as its years increase.

Its beginnings are no measure of its capabilities, nor

of its scope. At first no one knows what it is, or what it is worth. It remains perhaps for a time quiescent; it tries, as it were, its limbs, and proves the ground under it, and feels its way. From time to time, it makes essays which fail, and are in consequence abandoned. It seems in suspense which way to go; it wavers, and at length strikes out in one definite direction. In time it enters upon strange territory; points of controversy alter their bearing; parties rise and fall around it; dangers and hopes appear in new relations; and old principles reappear under new forms. It changes with them in order to remain the same. In a higher world it is otherwise, but here below to live is to change, and to be perfect is to have changed often. (*D. Ch. D.*, p. 39f.)

[WHAT would be the thoughts of a man who,] when examining a flower, or a herb, or a pebble, or a ray of light, which he treats as something so beneath him in the scale of existence, suddenly discovered that he was in the presence of some powerful being who was hidden behind the visible things he was inspecting,—who, though concealing his wise hand, was giving them their beauty, grace, and perfection, as being God's instrument for the purpose,—nay, whose robe and ornaments those objects were, which he was so eager to analyze? (*P. P. S.* II. 364)

WE PROCEED as far indeed as we can, by the logic of language, but we are obliged to supplement it by the more subtle and elastic logic of thought; for forms by themselves prove nothing. (*G. of A.*, p. 359)

CLEARNESS in argument certainly is not indispensable to reasoning well. Accuracy in stating doctrines or principles is not essential to feeling and acting upon them. The exercise of analysis is not necessary to the integrity of the process analyzed. The process of reasoning is complete in itself, and independent. (*O. U. S.*, p. 259)

WE ARE accustomed to point to the rise and spread of Christianity as a miraculous fact, and rightly so, on account of the weakness of its instruments, and the appalling weight and multiplicity of the obstacles which confronted it. To clear away those obstacles was to move mountains; yet this was done by a few poor, obscure, unbefriended men, and their poor, obscure, unbefriended followers. No social movement can come up to this marvel, which is singular and archetypical, certainly; it is a Divine work, and we soon cease to admire it in order to adore. But there is more in it than its own greatness to contemplate; it is so great as to be prolific of greatness. Those whom it has created, its children who have become such by a supernatural power, have imitated, in their own acts, the dispensation which made them what they were; and, though they have not carried out works simply miraculous, yet they have done exploits sufficient to bespeak their own unearthly origin, and the new powers which had come into the world. The revival of letters by the energy of Christian ecclesiastics and laymen, when everything had to be done, reminds us of the birth of Christianity itself, as far as a work of man can resemble a work of God. (*H. S.* III. 164)

NO truth can really exist external to Christianity. (*O. U. S.*, p. 309)

THE world overcomes us, not merely by appealing to our reason, or by exciting our passions, but by imposing on our imagination. (*O. U. S.*, p. 122)

IT IS well to have rich architecture, curious works of art, and splendid vestments, when you have a present God; but oh! what a mockery, if you have not! Thus your Church becomes, not a home, but a sepulchre; like those high cathedrals, once Catholic, which you do not know what to do with, which you shut up and make monuments of, sacred to the memory of what has passed away. (*A. D.* 1. 225)

HEREIN is the strength of the Catholic Church; herein she differs from all Protestant mockeries of her. She professes to be built upon facts, not opinions; on objective truths, not on variable sentiments; on immemorial testimony, not on private judgment; on convictions or perceptions, not on conclusions. None else but she can make this profession. She makes high claims against the temporal power, but she has that within her which justifies her. She merely acts out what she says she is. She does no more than she reasonably should do. If God has given her a specific work, no wonder she is not under the superintendence of the civil magistrate in doing it. If her Clergy be Priests, if they can forgive sins, and bring the Son of God upon her altars, it is obvious they cannot, considered as such, hold of the State. (*A. D.* 1. 216f.)

MANY a man is acting on utilitarian principles, who is shocked at them in set treatises, and disowns them. (*O. U. S.*, p. 325)

IN EVERYTHING there is a better side and a worse; in every place a disreputable set and a respectable, and the one is hardly known at all to the other. Men come away from the same University at this day, with contradictory impressions and contradictory statements, according to the society they have found there; if you believe the one, nothing goes on there as it should be: if you believe the other, nothing goes on as it should *not*. (*H. S.* III. 44)

REASON can but ascertain the profound difficulties of our condition, it cannot remove them; it has no work, it makes no beginning, it does but continually fall back, till it is content to be a little child, and to follow where Faith guides it. (*O. U. S.*, p. 351)

O MOTHER of saints! * O school of the wise! O nurse of the heroic! Of whom went forth, in whom have dwelt, memorable names of old, to spread the truth abroad, or to cherish and illustrate it at home! O thou, from whom surrounding nations lit their lamps! O virgin of Israel! wherefore dost thou now sit on the ground and keep silence, like one of the foolish women who were without oil on the coming of the Bridegroom? Where is now the ruler in Zion, and the doctor in the Temple, and the ascetic on Carmel, and the herald in the wilderness, and the preacher in the market-place? where are thy "effectual fervent prayers," offered in secret, and thy alms and good works coming up as a memorial before God?

O my mother, whence is this unto thee, that thou hast

* The Church of England to which Newman is here bidding farewell before becoming a Catholic.

good things poured out upon thee and canst not keep them, and bearest children, yet darest not own them? why hast thou not the skill to use their services, nor the heart to rejoice in their love? how is it that whatever is generous in purpose, and tender or deep in devotion, thy flower and thy promise, falls from thy bosom, and finds no home within thine arms? Who hath put this note upon thee, to have a "miscarrying womb, and dry breasts," to be strange to thine own flesh, and thine eye cruel towards thy little ones?

Thine own offspring, the fruit of thy womb, who love thee and would toil for thee, thou dost gaze upon them with fear, as though a portent, or thou dost loathe as an offense;—at best thou dost but endure, as if they had no claim but on thy patience, self-possession, and vigilance, to be rid of them as easily as thou mayest. Thou makest them "stand all the day idle," as the very condition of thy bearing with them; or thou biddest them be gone, where they will be more welcome; or thou sellest them for nought to the stranger that passes by. And what wilt thou do in the end thereof? (*S. S. D.,* p. 406ff.)

WHAT is the main guide of the soul, given to the whole race of Adam, outside the true fold of Christ as well as within it, given from the first dawn of reason, given to it in spite of that grievous penalty of ignorance which is one of the chief miseries of our fallen state? It is the light of conscience, "the true Light," as the Evangelist says, "which lighteth every man that cometh into the world." Whether a man be born in pagan darkness, or in some corruption of revealed religion; whether he has heard the Name of the Saviour of the world or not;

whether he be the slave of some superstition, or is in possession of some portions of Scripture, in any case, he has within his breast a certain commanding dictate, not a mere sentiment, not a mere opinion, or impression, or view of things, but a law, an authoritative voice, bidding him do certain things and avoid others. It is more than a man's self. The man himself has not power over it, or only with extreme difficulty; he did not make it, he cannot destroy it. He may silence it in particular cases or directions; he may distort its enunciations; but he cannot—or it is quite the exception if he can—he cannot emancipate himself from it. He can disobey it, he may refuse to use it; but it remains.

This is Conscience; and, from the nature of the case, its very existence carries on our minds to a Being exterior to ourselves; else, whence its strange, troublesome peremptoriness? I say its very existence throws us out of ourselves, and beyond ourselves, to go and seek for Him in the height and depth, whose voice it is. As the sunshine implies that the sun is in the heavens, though we may see it not; as a knocking at our doors at night implies the presence of one outside in the dark who asks for admittance, so this Word within us necessarily raises our minds to the idea of a Teacher, an unseen Teacher. (*S. V. O.*, p. 64f.)

[CONSCIENCE] holds of God, and not of man, as an Angel walking on the earth would be no citizen or dependent of the Civil Power. Conscience is not a long-sighted selfishness, nor a desire to be consistent with oneself! but it is a messenger from Him, who, both in nature and in grace, speaks to us behind a veil, and teaches and rules us by His representatives. Conscience is the aboriginal Vicar of Christ, a prophet in its informations, a monarch in its peremptoriness, a priest in its blessings, and anathemas, and, even though the eternal priesthood throughout the Church could cease to be, in it the sacerdotal principle would remain and would have a sway.

Words such as these are idle empty verbiage to the great world of philosophy now. All through my days there has been a resolute warfare, I had almost said conspiracy against the rights of conscience, as I have described it. Literature and science have been embodied in great institutions in order to put it down. Noble buildings have been reared as fortresses against that spiritual, invisible influence which is too subtle for science and too profound for literature. Chairs in Universities have been made the seats of an antagonist tradition. Public writers, day by day, have indoctrinated the minds of innumerable readers with theories subversive of its claims.

As in Roman times, and in the middle age, its supremacy was assailed by the arm of physical force, so now the intellect is put in operation to sap the foundations of a power which the sword could not destroy. We are told that conscience is but a twist in primitive and untutored man; that its dictate is an imagination; that the very notion of guiltiness, which that dictate enforces, is simply irrational, for how can there possibly be freedom of will, how can there be consequent responsibility, in that infinite eternal network of cause and effect, in which we helplessly lie? and what retribution have we to fear, when we have had no real choice to do good or evil?

When men advocate the rights of conscience, they in no sense mean the rights of the Creator, nor the duty to Him, in thought and deed, of the creature; but the right of thinking, speaking, writing, and acting, according to their judgment or their humour, without any thought of God at all. They do not even pretend to go by any moral rule, but they demand for each to be his own master in all things, and to profess what he pleases, asking no one's leave, and accounting priest or preacher, speaker or writer, unutterably impertinent, who dares to say a word against his going to perdition, if he like it, in his own way.

Conscience has rights because it has duties; but in this age, with a large portion of the public, it is the very right and freedom of conscience to dispense with conscience, to ignore a Lawgiver and Judge, to be independent of unseen obligations. It becomes a license to take up any or no religion, to take up this or that and let it go again, to go to church, to go to chapel, to boast of being above all religions and to be an impartial critic of each of them. Conscience is a stern monitor, but in this century it has been superseded by a counterfeit, which the eighteen centuries prior to it never heard of, and could not have mistaken for it, if they had. It is the right of self-will. (*A. D.* II. 248ff.)

I SPOKE of the scorn and hatred which a cultivated mind feels for some kinds of vice, and the utter disgust and profound humiliation which may come over it, if it should happen in any degree to be betrayed into them. Now this feeling may have its root in faith and love, but it may not; there is nothing really religious in it, considered by itself. Conscience indeed is implanted in the breast by nature, but it inflicts upon us fear as well as shame; when the mind is simply angry with itself and nothing more, surely the true import of the voice of

nature and the depth of its intimations have been forgotten, and a false philosophy has misinterpreted emotions which ought to lead to God. Fear implies the
transgression of a law, and a law implies a lawgiver and
judge; but the tendency of intellectual culture is to swal-
low up the fear in the self-reproach, and self-reproach
is directed and limited to our mere sense of what is
fitting and becoming. Fear carries us out of ourselves,
shame confines us within the round of our own thoughts.
Such, I say, is the danger which awaits a civilized age;
such is its besetting sin (not inevitable, God forbid! or
we must abandon the use of God's own gifts), but still
the ordinary sin of the Intellect; conscience becomes what
is called a moral sense; the command of duty is a sort of
taste; sin is not an offence against God, but against
human nature. (*I. of U.*, p. 191)

AS SOON as [man] has secured for himself some little
cultivation of intellect, he looks about him how he can
manage to dispense with Conscience, and find some other
principle to do its work. The most plausible and obvious
and ordinary of these expedients, is the Law of the
State, human law; the more plausible and ordinary, because it really comes to us with a divine sanction, and
necessarily has a place in every society or community of
men. Accordingly it is very widely used instead of Conscience, as but a little experience of life will show us;
"the law says this;" "would you have me go against
the law?" is considered an unanswerable argument in
every case; and, when the two come into collision, it follows of course that Conscience is to give way, and the
Law to prevail.

Another substitute for Conscience is the rule of Expediency: Conscience is pronounced superannuated and retires on a pension, whenever a people is so far advanced in illumination, as to perceive that right and wrong can to a certain extent be measured and determined by the useful on the one hand, and by the hurtful on the other; according to the maxim, which embodies this principle, that "honesty is the best policy."

Another substitute of a more refined character is the principle of Beauty:—it is maintained that the Beautiful and the Virtuous mean the same thing, and are convertible terms. Accordingly Conscience is found out to be but slavish; and a fine taste, an exquisite sense of the decorous, the graceful, and the appropriate, this is to be our true guide for ordering our mind and our conduct, and bringing the whole man into shape. These are great sophisms, it is plain; for, true though it be, that virtue is always expedient, always fair, it does not therefore follow that every thing which is expedient, and every thing which is fair, is virtuous. A pestilence is an evil, yet may have its undeniable uses; and war, "glorious war," is an evil, yet an army is a very beautiful object to look upon; and what holds in these cases, may hold in others; so that it is not very safe or logical to say that Utility and Beauty are guarantees for Virtue. (*H. S.* III. 79f.)

WHAT is the world's religion now? It has taken the brighter side of the Gospel,—its tidings of comfort, its precepts of love; all darker, deeper views of man's condition and prospects being comparatively forgotten. This is the religion *natural* to a civilised age, and well has Satan dressed and completed it into an idol of the Truth. As the reason is cultivated, the taste formed, the affections and sentiments refined, a general decency and grace will of course spread over the face of society, quite independently of the influence of Revelation. That beauty and delicacy of thought, which is so attractive in books, then extends to the conduct of life, to all we have, all we do, all we are. Our manners are courteous; we avoid giving pain or offence; our words become correct; our relative duties are carefully performed. Our sense of propriety shows itself even in our domestic arrangements, in the embellishments of our houses, in our amusements, and so also in our religious profession. Vice now becomes unseemly and hideous to the imagination, or, as it is sometimes familiarly said, "out of taste."

Thus elegance is gradually made the test and standard of virtue, which is no longer thought to possess an intrinsic claim on our hearts, or to exist, *further than* it leads to the quiet and comfort of others. Conscience is no longer recognised as an independent arbiter of actions, its authority is explained away; partly it is superseded in the minds of men by the so-called moral sense, which is regarded merely as the love of the beautiful; partly by the rule of expediency, which is forthwith substituted for it in the details of conduct. Now conscience is a stern, gloomy principle; it tells us of guilt and of prospective punishment. Accordingly, when its terrors disappear, then disappear also, in the creed of the day, those fearful images of Divine wrath with which the Scriptures abound. They are explained away. Everything is bright and cheerful. Religion is pleasant and easy; benevolence is the chief virtue; intolerance, bigotry, excess of zeal, are the first of sins. Austerity is an absurdity;—even firmness is looked on with an unfriendly, suspicious eye.

On the other hand, all open profligacy is discountenanced; drunkenness is accounted a disgrace; cursing and swearing are vulgarities. Moreover, to a cultivated mind, which recreates itself in the varieties of literature and knowledge, and is interested in the ever-accumulating discoveries of science, and the ever-fresh accessions of information, political or otherwise, from foreign countries, religion will commonly seem to be dull, from want of novelty. Hence excitements are eagerly sought out and rewarded. New objects in religion, new systems and plans, new doctrines, new preachers, are necessary to satisfy that craving which the so-called spread of knowledge has created. The mind becomes morbidly sensitive and fastidious; dissatisfied with things as they are, desirous of a change *as such,* as if alteration must of itself be a relief. (*P. P. S.* 1. 311ff.)

[IN the case of certain men] Conscience has been silenced. The only information they have received concerning God has been from Natural Theology, and that speaks only of benevolence and of harmony. They argue that it is our duty to solace ourselves here (in moderation, of course) with the goods of this life,—that we have only to be thankful while we use them,—that we need not alarm ourselves,—that God is a merciful God,—that amendment is quite sufficient to atone for our offences,— that though we have been irregular in our youth, yet that is a thing gone by,—that we forget it, and therefore God forgets it,—that the world is, on the whole, very well disposed towards religion,—that we should avoid enthusiasm,—that we should not be over-serious,—that we should have large views on the subject of human nature,—and that we should love all men. This indeed is the creed of shallow men in *every* age. (*P. P. S.* 1. 319)

[IT] WAS the quarrel of the ancient heathen with Christianity, that, instead of simply fixing the mind on the fair and the pleasant, it intermingled other ideas with them of a sad and painful nature; that it spoke of tears before joy, a cross before a crown; that it laid the foundation of heroism in penance; that it made the soul tremble with the news of purgatory and hell; that it insisted on views and a worship of the Deity which to their minds was nothing else than mean, servile and cowardly. The notion of an All-perfect, Ever-present God, in whose sight we are less than atoms, and who, while He deigns to visit us, can punish as well as bless, was abhorrent to them. They made their own minds their sanctuary, their own ideas their oracle, and conscience in morals was but parallel to genius and art and wisdom in philosophy. . . . Accordingly, virtue being only one kind of beauty, the principle which determines what is virtuous is—not conscience, but—taste. (*I. of U.*, p. 193ff.)

SUCH a doctrine is essentially superficial, and such will be its effects. It has no better measure of right and wrong than that of visible beauty and tangible fitness. Conscience, indeed, inflicts an acute pang, but that pang, forsooth, is irrational, and to reverence it is an illiberal superstition. But, if we will make light of what is deepest within us, nothing is left but to pay homage to what is more on the surface. To *seem* becomes to be; what looks fair will be good, what causes offence will be evil, virtue will be what pleases, vice what pains. As well may we measure virtue by utility as by such a rule. Nor is this an imaginary apprehension; we all must recollect the celebrated sentiment into which a great and wise man was betrayed in the glowing eloquence of his valediction to the spirit of chivalry.

"It is gone," cries Mr. Burke; "that sensibility of principle, that chastity of honour, which felt a stain like a wound; which inspired courage while it mitigated ferocity; which ennobled whatever it touched, and under which *vice lost half its evil by losing all its grossness*." In the last clause of this beautiful sentence we have too apt an ilustration of the ethical temperament of a civilised age. It is detection, not the sin, which is the crime; private life is sacred and inquiry into it is intolerable; and decency is virtue. Scandals, vulgarities, whatever shocks, whatever disgusts, are offences of the first order. Drinking and swearing, squalid poverty, improvidence, laziness, slovenly disorder, make up the idea of profligacy; poets may say anything, however wicked, with impunity; works of genius may be read without danger or shame, whatever be their principles; fashion, celebrity, the beautiful, the heroic, will suffice to force any evil upon the community. The splendours of a court and the charms of good society, wit, imagination, taste and high breeding, the *prestige* of rank and the resources of wealth, are a screen, an instrument and an apology for vice and irreligion. And thus at length we find, surprising as the change may be, that that very refinement of intellectualism, which began by repelling sensuality, ends by excusing it. (*I. of U.*, p. 201f.)

YOU do not get rid of vice by human expedients. You must go to a higher source for renovation of the heart and of the will. You do but play a sort of "hunt the slipper" with the fault of our nature, till you go to Christianity. (*D. and A.*, p. 273f.)

MANY persons are very sensitive of the difficulties of religion. I am as sensitive of them as any one, but I have never been able to see a connection between apprehending those difficulties, however keenly, and multiplying them to any extent, and, on the other hand, doubting the doctrines to which they are attached. Ten thousand difficulties do not make one doubt, as I understand the subject; difficulty and doubt are incommensurate. There of course may be difficulties in the evidence, but I am speaking of difficulties intrinsic to the doctrines themselves, or to their relations with each other. A man may be annoyed that he cannot work out a mathematical problem, of which the answer is or is not given him, without doubting that it admits of an answer, or that a certain particular answer is the true one. Of all points of faith, the being of a God is, to my own apprehension, encompassed with most difficulty, and yet borne in upon our minds with most power. (*Apol.*, p. 331f.)

SCRIPTURE is a refuge in any trouble; only let us be on our guard against seeming to use it further than is fitting, or doing more than sheltering ourselves under its shadow. Let us use it according to our measure. It is far higher and wider than our need; and its language veils our feelings while it gives expression to them. It is sacred and heavenly; and it restrains and purifies, while it sanctions them. (*S. S. D.*, p. 408)

[HURRELL FROUDE] was a man of the highest gifts,—so truly many-sided, that it would be presumptuous in me to attempt to describe him, except under those aspects in which he came before me. Nor have I here to speak of the gentleness and tenderness of nature, the playfulness, the free elastic force and graceful versatility of mind, and the patient winning considerateness in discussion, which endeared him to those to whom he opened his heart.

I speak of Hurrell Froude in his intellectual aspect, as a man of high genius, brimful and overflowing with ideas and views, in him original, which were too many and strong even for his bodily strength, and which crowded and jostled against each other in their effort after distinct shape and expression. And he had an intellect as critical and logical as it was speculative and bold. Dying prematurely, as he did, and in the conflict and transition-state of opinion, his religious views never reached their ultimate conclusion, by the very reason of their multitude and their depth. His opinions arrested and influenced me, even when they did not gain my assent. He professed openly his admiration of the Church of Rome, and his hatred of the Reformers.

He had a keen insight into abstract truth; but he was an Englishman to the backbone in his severe adherence to the real and the concrete. He had a most classical taste, and a genius for philosophy and art; and he was fond of historical inquiry, and the politics of religion. He had no turn for theology as such. He set no sufficient value on the writings of the Fathers, on the detail or development of doctrine, on the definite traditions of the Church viewed in their matter, on the teaching of the Ecumenical Councils, or on the controversies out of which they arose.

He took an eager courageous view of things on the whole. His power of entering into the minds of others did not equal his other gifts; he could not believe, for instance, that I really held the Roman Church to be Antichristian. On many points he would not believe but that I agreed with him, when I did not. He seemed not to understand my difficulties. His were of a different kind, the contrariety between theory and fact.

He taught me to look with admiration towards the Church of Rome, and in the same degree to dislike the Reformation. He fixed deep in me the idea of devotion to the Blessed Virgin, and he led me gradually to believe in the Real Presence. (*Apol.*, p. 125ff.)

WHO was the first cultivator of corn? Who first tamed and domesticated the animals whose strength we use, and whom we make our food? Or who first discovered the medicinal herbs which, from the earliest times, have been our resource against disease? If it was mortal man, who thus looked through the vegetable and animal worlds, and discriminated between the useful and the worthless, his name is unknown to the millions whom he has benefited. It is notorious, that those who first suggest the most happy inventions, and open a way to the secret stores of nature,—those who weary themselves in the search after Truth, who strike out momentous principles of action, who painfully force upon their contemporaries the adoption of beneficial measures, or, again, who are the original cause of the chief events in national history, are commonly supplanted, as regards celebrity and reward, by inferior men. Their works are not called after them; nor the arts and systems which they have given to the world. Their schools are usurped by strangers; and their maxims of wisdom circulate among the children of their people, forming, perhaps, a nation's character, but not embalming in their own immortality the names of their original authors. (*P. P. S.* II. 5f.)

GREAT minds need elbow-room, not indeed in the domain of faith, but of thought. (*I. of U.*, p. 476)

ERROR may flourish for a time, but Truth will prevail in the end. The only effect of error ultimately is to promote Truth. (*I. of U.*, p. 478)

BAD company creates a distaste for good; and hence it happens that when a youth has gone the length I have been supposing, he is repelled, from that very distaste, from those places and scenes which would do him good. He begins to lose the delight he once had in going home. By little and little he loses his enjoyment in the pleasant countenances, and untroubled smiles, and gentle ways, of that family circle which is so dear to him still. At first he says to himself that he is not worthy of them, and therefore keeps away; but at length the routine of home is tiresome to him. He has aspirations and ambitions which home does not satisfy. He wants more than home can give. His curiosity now takes a new turn; he listens to views and discussions which are inconsistent with the sanctity of religious faith.

At first he has no temptation to adopt them; only he wishes to know what is "said." As time goes on, however, living with companions who have no fixed principle, and who, if they do not oppose, at least do not take for granted, any the most elementary truth; or worse, hearing or reading what is directly against religion, at length, without being conscious of it, he admits a sceptical influence upon his mind. He does not know it, he does not recognise it, but there it is; and, *before* he recognises it, it leads him to a fretful, impatient way of speaking of the persons, conduct, words, and measures of religious men or of men in authority. This is the way in which he relieves his mind of the burden which is growing heavier and heavier every day. And so he goes on, approximating more and more closely to sceptics and infidels, and feeling more and more congeniality with their modes of thinking, till some day suddenly, from some accident, the fact breaks upon him, and he sees clearly that he is an unbeliever himself. (*S. V. O.*, p. 10f.)

NO ONE really loves another who does not feel a certain reverence towards him. When friends transgress this sobriety of affection, they may indeed continue associates for a time, but they have broken the bond of union. It is a mutual respect which makes friendship lasting. (*P. P. S.* I. 304)

LITERATURE is almost in its essence unreal; for it is the exhibition of thought disjoined from practice. Its very home is supposed to be ease and retirement; and when it does more than speak or write, it is accused of transgressing its bounds. This indeed constitutes what is considered its true dignity and honour, viz. its abstraction from the actual affairs of life; its security from the world's currents and vicissitudes; its saying without doing. A man of literature is considered to preserve his dignity by doing nothing; and when he proceeds forward into action, he is thought to lose his position, as if he were degrading his calling by enthusiasm, and becoming a politician or a partisan. Hence mere literary men are able to say strong things against the opinions of their age, whether religious or political, without offence, because no one thinks they mean anything by them. They are not expected to go forward to act upon them, and mere words hurt no one. (*P. P. S.* v. 42)

[THERE is an] endemic perennial fidget which possesses us about giving scandal; facts are omitted in great histories, or glosses are put upon memorable acts, because they are thought not edifying, whereas of all scandals such omissions, such glosses, are the greatest. (*H. S.* II. 231ff.)

IT IS as absurd to argue men, as to torture them, into believing. (*O. U. S.*, p. 63)

GREEK is celebrated for its copiousness in vocabulary, for its perspicuity, and its reproductive power; and its consequent facility of expressing the most novel or abstruse ideas with precision and elegance. Hence the Attic style of eloquence is plain and simple, because simplicity and plainness were not incompatible with clearness, energy, and harmony. In Greek, indeed, the words fall, as it were, naturally, into a distinct and harmonious order; and, from the exuberant richness of the materials, less is left to the ingenuity of the artist.

Latin is not a philosophical language, not a language in which a deep thinker is likely to express himself with purity or neatness. Cicero found it barren and dissonant, and as such he had to deal with it. His good sense enabled him to perceive what could be done, and what it was vain to attempt; and happily his talents answered precisely to the purpose required. He may be compared to a clever landscape gardener, who gives depth and richness to narrow and confined premises by ingenuity and skill in the disposition of his trees and walks. (*H. S.* I. 295ff.)

CICERO vividly realised the *status* of a Roman senator and statesman, and the "pride of place" of Rome, in all the grace and grandeur which attached to her; and he imbibed, and became, what he admired. As the exploits of Scipio or Pompey are the expression of this greatness in deed, so the language of Cicero is the expression of it in word. And, as the acts of the Roman ruler or soldier represent to us, in a manner special to themselves, the characteristic magnanimity of the lords of the earth, so do the speeches or treatises of her accomplished orator bring it home to our imaginations as no other writing could do. Neither Livy, nor Tacitus, nor Terence, nor Seneca, nor Pliny, nor Quintilian, is an adequate spokesman for the Imperial City. They write Latin; Cicero writes Roman. (*I. of U.*, p. 281f.)

WE SEE [Cicero] resigning his high station to Cato, who, with half his abilities, little foresight, and no address, possessed that first requisite for a statesman—firmness. Cicero, on the contrary, was irresolute, timid, and inconsistent. He talked, indeed, largely of preserving a middle course, but he was continually vacillating from one to the other extreme; always too confident or too dejected; incorrigibly vain of success, yet meanly panegyrising the government of a usurper. His foresight, sagacity, practical good sense, and singular tact, were lost for want of that strength of mind which points them steadily to one object. He was never decided, never (as has sometimes been observed) took an important step without afterwards repenting of it. (*H. S.* I. 251)

THE poems of Horace are most melancholy to read, but they bring before us most vividly and piteously our state by nature; they increase in us a sense of our utter dependence and natural helplessness; they arm us against the fallacious promises of the world, especially at this day—the promises of science and literature to give us light and liberty. Horace tries to solace himself with the pleasures of sense, and how stern a monitor he has within him, telling him that death is coming. (*Let.* II. 430)

WHEN I was fourteen or fifteen, I imitated Addison; when I was seventeen, I wrote in the style of Johnson; about the same time I fell in with the twelfth volume of Gibbon, and my ears rang with the cadences of his sentences, and I dreamed of it for a night or two. Then I began to make an analysis of Thucydides in Gibbon's style. (*I. of U.*, p. 322)

IT IS simply the fact that I have been obliged to take great pains with everything I have written, and I often write chapters over and over again, besides innumerable corrections and interleaved additions. I am not stating this as a merit, only that some persons write their best first, and I very seldom do. Those who are good speakers may be supposed to be able to write off what they want to say. I, who am not a good speaker, have to correct laboriously what I put on paper. However, I may truly say that I never have been in the practice, since I was a boy, of attempting to write well, or to form an elegant style. I think I never have written for writing's sake; but my one and single desire and aim has been to do what is so difficult, viz. to express clearly and exactly my meaning: this has been the motive principle of all my corrections and re-writings. When I have read over a passage which I had written a few days before, I have found it so obscure to myself that I have either put it altogether aside, or fiercely corrected it; for I don't get any better for practice. I am as much obliged to correct and re-write as I was thirty years ago.

As to patterns for imitation, the only master of style I have ever had (which is strange, considering the differences of the languages) is Cicero. I think I owe a great deal to him, and as far as I know to no one else. His great mastery of Latin is shown especially in his clearness. (*Let.* II. 426f.)

I WRITE to express the piercing sorrow that I feel in Thackeray's death. You know I never saw him, but you have interested me in him, and one saw in his books the workings of his mind—and he has died with such awful suddenness.

A new work of his had been advertised, and I had looked forward with pleasure to reading it; and now the drama of his life is closed, and he himself is the greatest instance of the text of which he was so full, *vanitas vanitatum, omnia vanitas.* I wonder whether he has known his own decay, for a decay I think there has been. I thought his last novel betrayed lassitude and exhaustion of mind, and he has lain by apparently for a year. His last (fugitive) pieces in the *Cornhill* have been almost sermons. One should be very glad to know that he had presentiments of what was to come. What a world is this! How wretched they are who take it for their portion! Poor Thackeray! it seems but the other day since we became Catholics; now all his renown has been since that—he has made his name, has been much made of, has been fêted, and has gone out, all since 1846 or 1847. (*Let.* ii. 428)

NOTHING is more common among men of a reasoning turn than to consider that no one reasons well but themselves. (*O. U. S.*, p. 209)

COURAGE does not consist in calculation, but in fighting against chances. (*O. U. S.*, p. 219)

GREAT objects exact a venture, and a sacrifice is the condition of honour. (*O. U. S.*, p. 220)

FROM the age of fifteen, dogma has been the fundamental principle of my religion: I know no other religion; I cannot enter into the idea of any other sort of religion; religion, as a mere sentiment, is to me a dream and a mockery. (*Apol.*, p. 150)

THERE is a great difference between a conclusion in the abstract and a conclusion in the concrete. A conclusion may be modified in fact by a conclusion from some opposite principle. (*Apol.*, p. 264)

I HAD a great dislike of paper logic. For myself, it was
not logic that carried me on; as well might one say that
the quicksilver in the barometer changes the weather.
It is the concrete being that reasons; pass a number of
years, and I find my mind in a new place; how? the
whole man moves; paper logic is but the record of it.

All the logic in the world would not have made me
move faster towards Rome than I did; as well might
you say that I have arrived at the end of my journey,
because I see the village church before me, as venture
to assert that the miles, over which my soul had to pass
before it got to Rome, could be annihilated, even though
I had had some far clearer view than I then had, that
Rome was my ultimate destination. Great acts take time.
(*Apol.*, p. 264f.)

THERE are but two alternatives, the way to Rome, and
the way to Atheism. (*Apol.*, p. 296)

OH, LOOK well to your footing that you slip not; be
very much afraid lest the world should detain you; dare
not in anything to fall short of God's grace, or to lag
behind when that grace goes forward. Walk with it,
co-operate with it, and I know how it will end. You
are not the first persons who have trodden that path;
yet a little time, and please God, the bitter shall be
sweet, and the sweet bitter, and you will have undergone
the agony, and will be lodged safely in the true home of
your souls and the valley of peace. Yet but a little while,
and you will look out from your resting-place upon the
wanderers outside; and will wonder why they do not
see that way which is now so plain to you, and will be

impatient with them that they do not come on faster. And, whereas you now are so perplexed in mind that you seem to yourselves to believe nothing, then you will be so full of faith, that you will almost see invisible mysteries, and will touch the threshold of eternity. (*A. D.* 1. 360f.)

WHAT a moment, when, breathless with the journey, and dizzy with the brightness, and overwhelmed with the strangeness of what is happening to him, and unable to realise where he is, the sinner [before the Judgment seat of Christ] hears the voice of the accusing spirit, bringing up all the sins of his past life, which he has forgotten, or which he has explained away, which he would not allow to be sins, though he suspected they were. And, oh! still more terrible, still more distracting, when the Judge speaks, and consigns the soul to the jailors, till it shall pay the endless debt which lies against it! "Impossible, I a lost soul! I separated from hope and from peace for ever! It is not I of whom the Judge so spake! There is a mistake somewhere: Christ, Saviour, hold Thy hand,—one minute to explain it! My name is Demas; I am but Demas, not Judas. What? hopeless pain! for me! impossible, it shall not be!"

Alas! poor soul; and while it thus fights with that destiny which it has brought upon itself, and with those companions whom it has chosen, the man's name is perhaps solemnly chanted forth, and his memory decently cherished among his friends on earth. His readiness in speech, his fertility in thought, his sagacity, or his wisdom, are not forgotten. Men talk of him from time to time; they appeal to his authority; they quote his words; perhaps they even raise a monument to his name, or write his history. "So comprehensive a mind! Such a power of throwing light on a perplexed subject, and bringing conflicting ideas or facts into harmony!" "Such a speech it was that he made on such and such an occasion; I happened to be present, and never shall forget it!" or, "It was the saying of a very sensible man"; or, "A great personage whom some of us knew"; or, "It was a rule with a very excellent and sensible friend of mine, now no more"; or, "Never was his equal in society, so just in his remarks, so versatile, so unobtrusive"; or, "I was fortunate to see him once when I was a boy"; or, "So great a benefactor to his country and his kind"; "His discoveries so great"; or, "His philosophy so profound." Oh, vanity! vanity of vanities, all is vanity! What profiteth it? What profiteth it? His soul is in hell. (*D. M. C.*, p. 38ff.)

AS FAR as, and wherever Love is wanting, so far, and there, Faith runs into excess or is perverted. (*O. U. S.*, p. 239)

ALL men have a reason, but not all men can give a reason. (*O. U. S.*, p. 259)

TRUE philosophy admits of being carried out to any extent; it is its very test, that no knowledge can be submitted to it with which it is not commensurate, and which it cannot annex to its territory. (*O. U. S.*, p. 309)

TRUE Catholicity is commensurate with the wants of the human mind; but persons are often to be found who are surprised that they cannot persuade all men to follow them, and cannot destroy dissent, by preaching a portion of the Divine system, instead of the whole of it. (*O. U. S.*, p. 310)

HERE is the badge of heresy: its dogmas are unfruitful; it has no theology. Deduct its remnant of Catholic theology, and what remains? Polemics, explanations, protests. (*O. U. S.*, p. 318)

CATHOLIC dogmas are, after all, but symbols of a Divine fact, which, far from being compassed by those very propositions, would not be exhausted, nor fathomed, by a thousand. (*O. U. S.*, p. 332)

KNOWLEDGE is the possession of those living ideas of sacred things, from which alone change of heart or conduct can proceed. (*O. U. S.*, p. 332)

[SOCIETY] begins in the poet and ends in the policeman. Universities are instances of the same course: they begin in Influence, they end in System. (*H. S.* III. 77)

HISTORY is at this day undergoing a process of revolution; the science of criticism, the disinterment of antiquities, the unrolling of manuscripts, the interpretation of inscriptions, have thrown us into a new world of thought; characters and events come forth transformed in the process; romance, prejudice, local tradition, party bias, are no longer accepted as guarantees of truth; the order and mutual relation of events are readjusted; the springs and the scope of action are reversed. Were Christianity a mere work of man, it, too, might turn out something different from what it has hitherto been considered; its history might require re-writing, as the history of Rome, or of the earth's strata, or of languages, or of chemical action.

A Catholic neither deprecates nor fears such inquiry, though he abhors the spirit in which it is too often conducted. He is willing that infidelity should do its work against the Church, knowing that she will be found just where she was, when the assault is over. It is nothing to him, though her enemies put themselves to the trouble of denying everything that has hitherto been taught, and begin with constructing her history all over again, for he is quite sure that they will end at length with a compulsory admission of what at first they so wantonly discarded. (*A. D.* I. 156f.)

HE WHO believes Revelation with that absolute faith which is the prerogative of a Catholic, is not the nervous creature who startles at every sudden sound, and is fluttered by every strange or novel appearance which meets his eyes. He has no sort of apprehension, he laughs at the idea that anything can be discovered by any other scientific method which can contradict any one of the dogmas of his religion. He knows full well there is no science whatever, but, in the course of its extension, runs the risk of infringing, without any meaning of offence on its own part, the path of other sciences: and he knows also that, if there be any one science which, from its sovereign and unassailable position can calmly bear such unintentional collisions on the part of the children of earth, it is Theology. He is sure, and nothing shall make him doubt, that, if anything seems to be proved by astronomer, or geologist, or chronologist, or antiquarian, or ethnologist, in contradiction to the dogmas of faith, that point will eventually turn out, first, *not* to be proved, or secondly, not *contradictory*, or thirdly, not contradictory to anything *really revealed*, but to something which has been confused with revelation. (*I. of U.*, p. 466f.)

THE great principles of the State are those of the Church, and, if the State would but keep within its own province, it would find the Church its truest ally and best benefactor. She upholds obedience to the magistrate; she recognises his office as from God; she is the preacher of peace, the sanction of law, the first element of order, and the safeguard of morality, and that without possible vacillation or failure; she may be fully trusted; she is a sure friend, for she is indefectible and undying. (*A. D. I.* 175)

THE promptitude, decisiveness, keenness, and force of the temporal power are well represented in the military host which is its instrument. Punctual in its movements, precise in its operations, imposing in its equipments, with its spirits high and its step firm, with its haughty clarion and its black artillery, behold, the mighty world is gone forth to war, with what? with an unknown something, which it feels but cannot see? which flits around it, which flaps against its cheek, with the air, with the wind. It charges and it slashes, and it fires its volleys, and its bayonets, and it is mocked by a foe who dwells in another sphere, and is far beyond the force of its analysis, or the capacities of its calculus. The air gives way, and it returns again; it exerts a gentle but constant pressure on every side; moreover, it is of vital necessity to the very power which is attacking it. Whom have you gone out against? a few old men, with red hats and stockings, or a hundred pale students, with eyes on the ground, and beads in their girdle; they are as stubble; destroy them;— then there will be other old men, and other pale students instead of them.

But we will direct our rage against one; he flees; what is to be done with him? Cast him out upon the wide world! but nothing can go on without him. Then bring him back! but he will give us no guarantee for the future. Then leave him alone; his power is gone, he is at an end, or he will take a new course of himself: he will take part with the State or the people. Meanwhile the multitude of interests in active operation all over the great Catholic body rise up, as it were, all around, and encircle the combat, and hide the fortune of the day from the eyes of the world; and unreal judgments are hazarded, and rash predictions, till the mist clears away, and then the old man is found in his own place, as before, saying Mass over the tomb of the Apostles. Resentment and animosity succeed in the minds of the many, when they find their worldly wisdom quite at fault, and that the weak has over-mastered the strong. They accuse the Church of craft. But, in truth, it is her very vastness, her manifold constituents, her complicated structure, which gives her this semblance, whenever she wears it, of feebleness, vacillation, subtleness, or dissimulation. She advances, retires, goes to and fro, passes to the right or left, bides her time, by a spontaneous, not a deliberate action. It is the divinely-intended method of her coping with the world's power. (*A. D.* I. 178f.)

FAITH is illuminative, not operative; it does not force obedience, though it increases responsibility; it heightens guilt, it does not prevent sin; the will is the source of action. (*A. D.* I. 286)

"BEFORE I got to the end [of my *Essay on the Development of Christian Doctrine*] I resolved to be received [into the Catholic Church], and the book remains in the state in which it was then, unfinished." The following is its final paragraph:

Such were the thoughts concerning the "Blessed Vision of Peace" of one whose long-continued petition had been that the Most Merciful would not despise the work of His own Hands, not leave him to himself;—while yet his eyes were dim, and his breast laden, and he could but employ Reason in the things of Faith. And now, dear Reader, time is short, eternity is long. Put not from you what you have here found; regard it not as mere matter of present controversy; set not out resolved to refute it, and looking about for the best way of doing so; seduce not yourself with the imagination that it comes of disappointment, or disgust, or restlessness, or wounded feelings, or undue sensibility, or other weakness. Wrap not yourself round in the associations of years past; nor determine that to be truth which you wish to be so, nor make an idol of cherished anticipations. Time is short, eternity is long.

NUNC DIMITTIS SERVUM TUUM, DOMINE,
SECUNDUM VERBUM TUUM IN PACE:
QUIA VIDERUNT OCULI MEI SALUTARE TUUM.

(*D. Ch. D.*, p. 445)

NOTORIETY, or, as it may be called, newspaper fame, is to the many what style and fashion, to use the language of the world, are to those who are within or belong to the higher circles; it becomes to them a sort of idol, worshipped for its own sake, and without any reference to the shape in which it comes before them. It may be an evil fame or a good fame; it may be the notoriety of a great statesman, or of a great preacher, or of a great speculator, or of a great experimentalist, or of a great criminal; of one who has laboured in the improvement of our schools, or hospitals, or prisons, or workhouses, or of one who has robbed his neighbour of his wife.

It matters not; so that a man is talked much of, and read much of, he is thought much of; nay, let him even have died justly under the hands of the law, still he will be made a sort of martyr of. His clothes, his handwriting, the circumstances of his guilt, the instruments of his deed of blood, will be shown about, gazed on, treasured up as so many relics; for the question with men is, not whether he is great, or good, or wise, or holy; not whether he is base, and vile, and odious, but whether he is in the mouths of men, whether he has centered on himself the attention of many, whether he has done something out of the way, whether he has been (as it were) canonised in the publications of the hour. "These are thy gods, O Israel!" (*D. M. C.*, p. 91f.)

EVERYTHING belonging to [Dives] was in the best style, as men speak; his house, his furniture, his plate of silver and gold, his attendants, his establishments. Everything was for enjoyment, and for show too; to attract the eyes of the world, and to gain the applause and admiration of his equals, who were the companions of his sins. These companions were doubtless such as became a person of such pretensions; they were fashionable men; a collection of refined, high-bred, haughty men, eating, not gluttonously, but what was rare and costly; delicate, exact, fastidious in their taste, from their very habits of indulgence; not eating for the mere sake of eating, or drinking for the mere sake of drinking, but making a sort of science of their sensuality; sensual, carnal, as flesh and blood can be, with eyes, ears, tongue, steeped in impurity, every thought, look, and sense, witnessing or ministering to the evil one who ruled them; yet with exquisite correctness of idea and judgment, laying down rules for sinning; —heartless and selfish, high, punctilious, and disdainful in their outward deportment, and shrinking from Lazarus, who lay at the gate, as an eye-sore, who ought for the sake of decency to be put out of the way.

Dives was one of such, and so he lived his short span, thinking of nothing, loving nothing, but himself, till one day he got into a fatal quarrel with one of his godless associates, or he caught some bad illness; and then he lay helpless on his bed of pain, cursing fortune and his physician, that he was no better, and impatient that he was thus kept from enjoying his youth, trying to fancy himself mending when he was getting worse, and disgusted at those who would not throw him some word of comfort in his suspense, and turning more resolutely from his Creator in proportion to his suffering;—and then at last his day came, and he died, and (oh! miserable!) "was buried in hell." And so ended he and his mission. (*D. M. C.*, p. 113f.)

BUT men who know but a little, are for that very reason most under the power of the imagination, which fills up for them at pleasure those departments of knowledge to which they are strangers; and, as the ignorance of abject minds shrinks from the spectres which it frames there, the ignorance of the self-confident is petulant and presuming. (*O. U. S.*, p. 68f.)

THE men commonly held in popular estimation are greatest at a distance; they become small as they are approached; but the attraction, exerted by unconscious holiness, is of an urgent and irresistible nature; it persuades the weak, the timid, the wavering, and the inquiring; it draws forth the affection and loyalty of all who are in a measure like-minded; and over the thoughtless or perverse multitude it exercises a sovereign compulsory sway, bidding them fear and keep silence, on the ground of its own right divine to rule them,—its hereditary claim on their obedience, though they understand not the principles or counsels of that spirit, which is "born, not of blood, nor of the will of the flesh, nor of the will of man, but of God." (*O. U. S.*, p. 95)

THOSE who have been brought up in ignorance of the polluting fashions of the world, too often feel a rising in their minds against the discipline and constraint kindly imposed upon them; and, not understanding that their ignorance is their glory, and that they cannot really enjoy both good and evil, they murmur that they are not allowed to essay what they do not wish to practise, or to choose for themselves in matters where the very knowledge seems to them to give a superiority to the children of corruption.

Thus the temptation of becoming as gods works as in the beginning, pride opening a door to lust; and then, intoxicated by their experience of evil, they think they possess real wisdom, and take a larger and more impartial view of the nature and destinies of man than religion teaches; and, while the customs of society restrain their avowals within the bounds of propriety, yet in their hearts they learn to believe that sin is a matter of course, not a serious evil, a failing in which all have share, indulgently to be spoken of, or rather, in the case of each individual, to be taken for granted, and passed over in silence; and believing this, they are not unwilling to discover or to fancy weaknesses in those who have the credit of being superior to the ordinary run of men, to insinuate the possibility of human passions influencing them, this or that of a more refined nature, when the grosser cannot be imputed, and, extenuating at the same time the guilt of the vicious, to reduce in this manner all men pretty much to a level. (*O. U. S.*, p. 125f.)

[THE world] assails the imagination [of Christians]. It sweeps by in long procession;—its principalities and powers, its Babel of language, the astrologers of Chaldæa, the horse and its rider and the chariots of Egypt, Baal and Ashtoreth and their false worship; and those who witness, feel its fascination; they flock after it; with a strange fancy, they ape its gestures, and dote upon its mummeries; and then, should they perchance fall in with the simple solemn services of Christ's Church, and hear her witnesses going the round of Gospel truths as when they left them: "I am the Way, the Truth, and the Life;" "Be sober, be vigilant;" "Strait is the gate, narrow the way;" "If any man will come after Me, let him deny himself;" "He is despised and rejected of men, a Man of sorrows and acquainted with grief:"—how utterly unreal do these appear, and the preachers of them, how irrational, how puerile!—how extravagant in their opinions, how weak in their reasoning!—and if they profess to pity and bear with them, how nearly does their compassion border on contempt! (*O. U. S.*, p. 132f.)

ETERNAL Truth, though at times it degenerates into superstition, is far better than that cold, sceptical, critical tone of mind, which has no inward sense of an over-rulling, ever-present Providence, no desire to approach its God, but sits at home waiting for the fearful clearness of His visible coming, whom it might seek and find in due measure amid the twilight of the present world. (*O. U. S.*, p. 220f.)

[THIS], then, under all circumstances, is real Faith: a presumption, yet not a mere chance conjecture,—a reaching forward, yet not of excitement or of passion,—a moving forward in the twilight, yet not without clue or direction;—a movement from something known to something unknown, but kept in the narrow path of truth by the Law of dutifulness which inhabits it, the Light of heaven which animates and guides it,—and which, whether feeble and dim as in the Heathen, or bright and vigorous as in the Christian, whether merely the awakening and struggling conscience, or the "affection of the Spirit," whether as a timid hope, or in the fulness of love, is, under every Dispensation, the one acceptable principle commending us to God for the merits of Christ. (*O. U. S.*, p. 249)

[THE Church] has scandals, she has a reproach, she has a shame: no Catholic will deny it. She has ever had the reproach and shame of being the mother of children unworthy of her. She has good children;—she has many more bad. Such is the will of God, as declared from the beginning. He might have formed a pure Church; but He has expressly predicted that the cockle, sown by the enemy, shall remain with the wheat, even to the harvest at the end of the world. He pronounced that His Church should be like a fisher's net, gathering of every kind, and not examined till the evening. Nay, more than this, He declared that the bad and imperfect should far surpass the good.

There is ever an abundance of materials in the lives and the histories of Catholics; ready to the use of those opponents who, starting with the notion that the Holy Church is the work of the devil, wish to have some corroboration of their leading idea. Her very prerogative gives special opportunity for it; I mean, that she is the Church of all lands and of all times. If there was a Judas among the Apostles, and a Nicholas among the deacons, why should we be surprised that in the course of eighteen hundred years, there should be flagrant instances of cruelty, of unfaithfulness, of hypocrisy, or of profligacy, and that not only in the Catholic people, but in high places, in royal palaces, in bishops' households, nay, in the seat of St. Peter itself?

Why need it surprise, if in barbarous ages, or in ages of luxury, there have been bishops, or abbots, or priests who have forgotten themselves and their God, and served the world or the flesh, and have perished in that evil service? What triumph is it, though in a long line of between two and three hundred popes, amid martyrs, confessors, doctors, sage rulers, and loving fathers of their people, one, or two, or three are found who fulfill the Lord's description of the wicked servant, who began "to strike the manservants and maidservants, and to eat and drink and be drunk"? I can only say that, taking man as he is, it would be a miracle were such offences altogether absent from her history. (*S. V. O.*, p. 144f.)

CERTITUDE is a point, but doubt is a progress. Certitude is a reflex action; it is to know that one knows. I believe I had not that, till close upon my reception into the Catholic Church. (*Apol.*, p. 307)

FEW minds in earnest can remain at ease without some sort of rational grounds for their religious belief; to reconcile theory and fact is almost an instinct of the mind. (*Apol.*, p. 351)

CATHOLICITY is not only one of the notes of the Church, but, according to the divine purposes, one of its securities. (*Apol.*, p. 359)

SCIENTIFIC knowledge is really growing, but it is by fits and starts; hypotheses rise and fall; it is difficult to anticipate which of them will keep their ground, and what the state of knowledge in relation to them will be from year to year. (*Apol.*, p. 353)

THE devotions to angels and saints as little interfere with the incommunicable glory of the Eternal, as the love which we bear our friends and relations, our tender human sympathies, are inconsistent with that supreme homage of the heart to the Unseen, which really does but sanctify and exalt what is of earth. (*Apol.*, p. 288f.)

TO ME nothing is so consoling, so piercing, so thrilling, so overcoming, as the Mass. It is not a mere form of words—it is a great action, the greatest action that can be on earth. It is, not the invocation merely, but, if I dare use the word, the evocation of the Eternal.

He becomes present on the altar in flesh and blood, before Whom angels bow and devils tremble. This is that awful event which is the end, and is the interpretation, of every part of the solemnity. Words are necessary, but as means, not as ends; they are not mere addresses to the throne of grace, they are instruments of what is far higher, of consecration, of sacrifice. They hurry on as if impatient to fulfil their mission. Quickly they go, the whole is quick, for they are all parts of one integral action. Quickly they go; for they are awful words of sacrifice, they are a work too great to delay upon; as when it was said in the beginning, "What thou doest, do quickly." Quickly they pass, for the Lord Jesus goes with them, as He passed along the lake in the days of His flesh, quickly calling first one and then another. Quickly they pass; because as the lightning which shineth from one part of the heaven unto the other, so is the coming of the Son of Man. Quickly they pass; for they are as the words of Moses, when the Lord came down in the cloud, calling on the Name of the Lord as He passed by, "The Lord, the Lord God, merciful and gracious, long-suffering, and abundant in goodness and truth." And as Moses on the mountain, so we too "make haste and bow our heads to the earth, and adore." (*L. and G.*, p. 327f.)

THE operation of the Holy Spirit has been calm, equable, gradual, far-spreading, over-taking, intimate, irresistible. What is so awfully silent, so mighty, so inevitable, so encompassing, as a flood of water? Fire alarms from the first: we see it, and we scent it; there is crashing and downfall, smoke and flame; it makes an inroad here and there; it is uncertain and wayward; but a flood is the reverse of all this. It gives no tokens of its coming; it lets men sleep through the night, and they wake and find themselves hopelessly besieged; prompt, secret, successful and equable, it preserves one level; it is everywhere; there is no refuge. And it makes its way to the foundations; towers and palaces rear themselves as usual; they have lost nothing of their perfection, and give no sign of danger, till at length suddenly they totter and fall. And here and there it is the same, as if by some secret understanding: for by one and the same agency the mighty movement goes on here and there and everywhere, and all things seem to act in concert with it, and to conspire together for their own ruin. And in the end they are utterly removed, and perish from off the face of the earth. Fire, which threatens more fiercely, leaves behind it relics and monuments of its agency; but water buries as well as destroys; it wipes off the memorial of its victims from the earth; it covers the chariot and the horsemen, and all the host of Pharaoh, and sweeps them away; "the waters overwhelm them, there is not one of them left." (*S. S. D.*, p. 128f.)

WHILE Reason and Revelation are consistent in fact, they often are inconsistent in appearance; and this seeming discordance acts most keenly and alarmingly on the Imagination, and may suddenly expose a man to the temptation, and even hurry him on to the commission, of definite acts of unbelief, in which reason itself really does not come into exercise at all.

Let a person devote himself to the studies of the day; let him be taught by the astronomer that our sun is but one of a million central luminaries, and our earth but one of ten million globes moving in space; let him learn from the geologist that on that globe of ours enormous revolutions have been in progress through innumerable ages; let him be told by the comparative anatomist of the minutely arranged system of organized nature; by the chemist and physicist, of the peremptory yet intricate laws to which nature, organized and inorganic, is subjected; by the ethnologist, of the originals, and ramifications, and varieties, and fortunes of nations; by the antiquarian, of old cities disinterred, and primitive countries laid bare, with the specific forms of human society once existing; by the linguist, of the slow formation and development of languages; by the psychologist, the physiologist, and the economist, of the subtle, complicated structure of the breathing, energetic, restless world of men; I say, let him take in and master the vastness of the view thus afforded him of nature, its infinite complexity, its awful comprehensiveness, and its diversified yet harmonious colouring; and then, when he has for years drunk in and fed upon this vision, let him turn round to peruse the inspired records, or listen to the authoritative teaching of Revelation, and he may certainly experience a most distressing revulsion of feeling,—not that his reason really deduces any thing from his much loved studies contrary to the faith, but that his imagination is bewildered, and swims with the sense of the ineffable distance of that faith from the view of things which is familiar to him, with its strangeness, and then again its rude simplicity, as he considers it, and its apparent poverty contrasted with the exuberant life and reality of his own world.

All this, the school I am speaking of understands well; it comprehends that, if it can but exclude the professors of Religion from the lecture-halls of science, it may safely allow them full play in their own; for it will be able to rear up infidels, without speaking a word, merely by the terrible influence of that faculty against which both Bacon and Butler so solemnly warn us.

I say, it leaves the theologian the full and free possession of his own schools, for it thinks he will have no chance of arresting the opposite teaching or of rivalling the fascination of modern science. Knowing little, and caring less for the depth and largeness of that heavenly Wisdom, on which the Apostle delights to expatiate, or the variety of those sciences, dogmatic or ethical, mystical or hagiological, historical or exegetical, which Revelation has created, these philosophers know perfectly well that, in matter of fact, to beings, constituted as we are, sciences which concern this world and this state of existence are worth far more, are more arresting and attractive, than those which relate to a system of things which they do not see and cannot master by their natural powers. Sciences which deal with tangible facts, practical results, evergrowing discoveries, and perpetual novelties, which feed curiosity, sustain attention, and stimulate expectation, require, they consider, but a fair stage and no favour to distance that Ancient Truth, which never changes. And therefore they look out for the day when they shall have put down Religion, not by shutting its schools, but by emptying them; not by disputing its tenets, but by the superior worth and persuasiveness of their own. (*I. of U.*, p. 401ff.)

IF THE very claim to infallible arbitration in religious disputes is of so weighty importance and interest in all ages of the world, much more is it welcome at a time like the present, when the human intellect is so busy, and thought so fertile, and opinion so indefinitely divided. The absolute need of a spiritual supremacy is at present the strongest of arguments in favour of its supply. Surely, either an objective revelation has not been given, or it has been provided with means for impressing its objectiveness on the world. If Christianity be a social religion, as it certainly is, and if it be based on certain ideas acknowledged as divine, or a creed, which shall here be assumed, and if these ideas have various aspects, and make distinct impressions on different minds, and issue in consequence in a multiplicity of developments, true, or false, what influence will suffice to meet and to do justice to these conflicting conditions, but a supreme authority ruling and reconciling individual judgments, by a divine right and a recognized wisdom? (*D. Ch. D.*, p. 89)

[INFALLIBILITY] claims, when brought into exercise in the legitimate manner, for otherwise of course it is but dormant, to have for itself a sure guidance into the very meaning of every portion of the Divine Message in detail, which was committed by our Lord to His Apostles. It claims to know its own limits, and to decide what it can determine absolutely and what it cannot. It claims, moreover, to have a hold upon statements not directly religious, so far as this,—to determine whether they indirectly relate to religion, and according to its own definitive judgment, to pronounce whether or not, in a particular case, they are consistent with revealed truth. It claims to decide magisterially, whether infallibly or not, that such and such statements are or are not prejudicial to the Apostolic *depositum* of faith, in their spirit or in their consequences, and to allow them, or condemn and forbid them, accordingly.

It claims to impose silence at will on any matters, of

controversies, of doctrine, which on its own *ipse dixit*, it pronounces to be dangerous, or inexpedient, or inopportune. It claims that, whatever may be the judgment of Catholics upon such acts, these acts should be received by them with those outward marks of reverence, submission, and loyalty, which Englishmen, for instance, pay to the presence of their sovereign, without public criticism on them, as being in their matter inexpedient, or in their manner violent or harsh. And lastly, it claims to have the right of inflicting spiritual punishment, of cutting off from the ordinary channels of the divine life, and of simply excommunicating, those who refuse to submit themselves to its formal declarations. Such is the infallibility lodged in the Catholic Church, viewed in the concrete, as clothed and surrounded by the appendages of its high sovereignty: it is, to repeat what I said above, a supereminent prodigious power sent upon earth to encounter and master a giant evil.

And now, having thus described it, I profess my own absolute submission to its claim. (*Apol.*, p. 341f.)

THERE is a time for every thing, and many a man desires a reformation of an abuse, or the fuller development of a doctrine, or the adoption of a particular policy, but forgets to ask himself whether the right time for it is come; and, knowing that there is no one who will do any thing towards it in his own lifetime unless he does it himself, he will not listen to the voice of authority, and spoils a good work in his own century, that another man, as yet unborn, may not bring it happily to perfection in the next. He may seem to the world to be nothing else than a bold champion for the truth and a martyr to free opinion, when he is just one of those persons whom the competent authority ought to silence, and, though the case may not fall within that subject-matter in which it is infallible, or the formal conditions of the exercise of that gift may be wanting, it is clearly the duty of authority to act vigorously in the case. Yet that act will go down to posterity as an instance of a tyrannical interference with private judgment, and of the silencing of a reformer, and of a base love of corruption or error. And all those who take the part of that ruling authority will be considered as time-servers, or indifferent to the cause of uprightness and truth. (*Apol.*, p. 350f.)

THERE never was a time when the intellect of the educated class was more active, or rather more restless, than in the middle ages. And then again all through Church history from the first, how slow is authority in interfering! Perhaps a local teacher, or a doctor in some local school, hazards a proposition, and a controversy ensues. It smoulders or burns in one place, no one interposing; Rome simply lets it alone. Then it comes before a Bishop; or some priest, or some professor in some other seat of learning takes it up; and then there is a second stage of it. Then it comes before a University, and it may be condemned by the theological faculty. So the controversy proceeds year after year, and Rome is still silent. An appeal perhaps is next made to a seat of authority inferior to Rome; and then at last after a long while it comes before the supreme power. Meanwhile, the question has been ventilated and turned over and over again, and viewed on every side of it, and authority is called upon to pronounce a decision, which has already been arrived at by reason. (*Apol.*, p. 357f.)

O HOW great a good will it be, if the time shall one day come, when we shall enter into His tabernacle above, and hide ourselves under the shadow of His wings; if we shall be in the number of those blessed dead who die in the Lord, and rest from their labour. Here we are tossing upon the sea, and the wind is contrary. All through the day we are tried and tempted in various ways. But in the unseen world, where Christ has entered, all is peace. "There is no more death, neither sorrow nor crying, neither any more pain; for the former things are passed away." Nor any more sin; nor any more guilt; no more remorse; no more punishment; no more penitence; no more trial; no infirmity to depress us; no affection to mislead us; no passion to transport us; no prejudice to blind us; no sloth, no pride, no envy, no strife; but the light of God's countenance, and a pure river of water of life, clear as crystal proceeding out of the Throne. That is our *home;* here we are but on pilgrimage, and Christ is calling us home. (*P. P. S.* VI. 232f.)

AT TIMES we seem to catch a glimpse of a Form which we shall hereafter see face to face. We approach, and in spite of the darkness, our hands, or our head, or our brow, or our lips become, as it were, sensible of the contact of something more than earthly. We know not where we are, but we have been bathing in water, and a voice tells us that it is blood. Or we have a mark signed upon our foreheads, and it spake of Calvary. Or we recollect a hand laid upon our heads, and surely it had the print of nails in it, and resembled His who with a touch gave sight to the blind and raised the dead. Or we have been eating and drinking; and it was not a dream surely, that One fed us from His wounded side, and renewed our nature by the heavenly meat He gave. (*P. P. S.* v. 10f.)

IN THE science of Education Protestants, depending on human means mainly, are led to make the most of them: their sole resource is to use what they have; "Knowledge is" their "power" and nothing else; they are the anxious cultivators of a rugged soil. It is otherwise with us. We have a goodly inheritance. This is apt to cause us—I do not mean to rely too much on prayer, and the Divine Blessing, for that is impossible, but we sometimes forget that we shall please Him best, and get most from Him, when, according to the Fable, we "put our shoulder to the wheel," when we use what we have by nature to the utmost, at the same time that we look out for what is beyond nature in the confidence of faith and hope. However, we are sometimes tempted to let things take their course, as if they would in one way or another turn up right at last for certain; and so we go on, living from hand to mouth, getting into difficulties and getting out of them, succeeding certainly on the whole, but with failure in detail which might be avoided, and with much of imperfection or inferiority in our appointments and plans, and much disappointment, discouragement, and collision of opinion in consequence. If this be in any measure the state of the case, there is certainly so far a reason for availing ourselves of the investigations and experience of those who are not Catholics, when we have to address ourselves to the subject of Liberal Education. (*I. of U.*, p. 5f.)

MAY the day come for all of us, cf which Easter is the promise, when that first spring may return to us, and a sweetness which cannot die may gladden our garden. (*Ward* II. 319*)

THE world, knowing nothing of the blessings of the Catholic faith, and prophesying nothing but ill concerning it, fancies that a convert, after the first fervour is over, feels nothing but disappointment, weariness, and offence in his new religion, and is secretly desirous of retracing his steps. This is at the root of the alarm and irritation which it manifests at hearing that doubts are incompatible with a Catholic's profession, because it is sure that doubts will come upon him, and then how pitiable will be his state!

That there can be peace, and joy, and knowledge, and freedom, and spiritual strength in the Church, is a thought far beyond [the world's] imagination; for it regards her simply as a frightful conspiracy against the happiness of man, seducing her victims by specious professions, and, when they are once hers, caring nothing for the misery which breaks upon them, so that by any means she may detain them in bondage. Accordingly, it conceives we are in perpetual warfare with our own reason, fierce objections ever rising within us, and we forcibly repressing them. It believes that, after the likeness of a vessel which has met with some accident at sea, we are ever bailing out the water which rushes in upon us, and have hard work to keep afloat; we just manage to linger on, either by an unnatural strain on our minds, or by turning them away from the subject of religion.

* From a letter to Helen Church.

The world disbelieves our doctrines itself, and cannot understand our own believing them. It considers them so strange, that it is quite sure, though we will not confess it, that we are haunted day and night with doubts, and tormented with the apprehension of yielding to them. It fancies that the reason is ever rebelling, like the flesh; that doubt, like concupiscence, is elicited by every sight and sound, and that temptation insinuates itself in every page of letter-press, and through the very voice of a Protestant polemic. When it sees a Catholic Priest, it looks hard at him, to make out how much there is of folly in his composition, and how much of hypocrisy. Trust me, rather than the world, when I tell you, that it is no difficult thing for a Catholic to believe; and that unless he grievously mismanages himself, the difficult thing is for him to doubt. (*D. M. C.*, p. 221f.)

IT IS the custom with Protestant writers to consider that, whereas there are two great principles in action in the history of religion, Authority and Private Judgment, they have all the Private Judgment to themselves, and we have the full inheritance and the superincumbent oppression of Authority. But this is not so; it is the vast Catholic body itself, and it only, which affords an arena for both combatants in that awful, never-dying duel. It is necessary for the very life of religion, viewed in its large operations and its history, that the warfare should be incessantly carried on. Every exercise of Infallibility is brought out into act by an intense and varied operation of the Reason, from within and without, and provokes again a re-action of Reason against it; and, as in a civil polity the State exists and endures by means of the rivalry and collision, the encroachments and defeats of its constituent parts, so in like manner Catholic Christendom is no simple exhibition of religious absolutism, but it presents a continuous picture of Authority and Private Judgment alternately advancing and retreating as the ebb and flow of the tide; it is a vast assemblage of human beings with wilful intellects and wild passions, brought together into one by the beauty and the majesty of a Superhuman Power—into what may be called a large reformatory or training-school, not to be sent to bed, not to be buried alive, but for the melting, refining, and moulding, as in some moral factory, by an incessant noisy process (if I may proceed to another metaphor), of the raw material of human nature, so excellent, so dangerous, so capable of divine purposes. (*Apol.*, p. 343f.)

THE very idea of the Catholic Church, as an instrument of supernatural grace, is that of an institution which innovates upon, or rather superadds to nature. She does something for nature above or beyond nature. When, then, it is said that she makes her members one, this implies that by nature they are not one, and would not become one. Left to himself, each Catholic likes and would maintain his own opinion and his private judgment just as much as a Protestant; and he has it, and he maintains it, just so far as the Church does not, by the authority of Revelation, supersede it. The very moment the Church ceases to speak, at the very point at which she, that is, God who speaks by her, circumscribes her range of teaching, there private judgment of necessity starts up; there is nothing to hinder it.

The intellect of man is active and independent: he forms opinions about everything; he feels no deference

for another's opinion, except in proportion as he thinks
that other is more likely than he to be right; and he
never absolutely sacrifices his own opinion, except when
he is sure that that other knows for certain. He *is* sure
that God knows; therefore, if he is a Catholic, he sacrifices his opinion to the Word of God, speaking through
His Church. But, from the nature of the case, there is
nothing to hinder his having his own opinion, and expressing it, whenever, and so far as, the Church, the
oracle of Revelation does not speak. (*A. D.*, I. § 300f.)

[THE Catholic] doctrines are members of one family,
and suggestive, or correlative, or confirmatory, or illustra-
tive of each other. In other words, one furnishes evidence
to another, and all to each of them; if this is proved,
that becomes probable; if this and that are both probable, but for different reasons, each adds to the other its
own probability. The Incarnation is the antecedent of
the doctrine of Mediation, and the archetype both of
the Sacramental principle, and of the merits of Saints.
From the doctrine of Mediation follow the Atonement,
the Mass, the merits of Martyrs and Saints, their invocation and cultus. From the Sacramental principle come
the Sacraments properly so called, the unity of the
Church, and the Holy See as its type and centre; the
authority of Councils; the sanctity of rites; the veneration of holy places, shrines, images, vessels, furniture, and
vestments.

Of the Sacraments, Baptism is developed into Con-
firmation on the one hand, into Penance, Purgatory, and
Indulgences, on the other; and the Eucharist into the
Real Presence, adoration of the Host, Resurrection of
the Body, and the virtue of Relics. Again, the doctrine

of the Sacraments leads to the doctrine of Justification;
Justification to that of Original Sin; Original Sin to
the merit of Celibacy. Nor do these separate developments stand independent of each other, but by cross
relations they are connected, and grow together while
they grow from one.

The Mass and Real Presence are parts of one; the
veneration of Saints and their Relics are parts of one;
their intercessory power, and the Purgatorial State, and,
again, the Mass and that State are correlative; Celibacy
is the characteristic mark of Monachism and the Priesthood. You must accept the whole, or reject the whole;
reduction does but enfeeble, and amputation mutilate.
It is trifling to receive all but something which is as
integral as any other portion; and, on the other hand,
it is a solemn thing to receive any part, for, before you
know where you are, you may be carried by a stern logical necessity to accept the whole. (*D. Ch. D.*, p. 93f.)

NATURE is one with nature, grace with grace; the world
then witnesses against you by being good friends with
you; you could not have got on with the world so well,
without surrendering something which was precious and
sacred. The world likes you, all but your professed creed;
distinguishes you from your creed in its judgment of
you, and would fain separate you from it in fact. Men
say, "These persons are better than their Church; we
have not a word to say for their Church; but Catholics
are not what they were; they are very much like other
men now. Their Creed certainly is bigoted and cruel, but
what would you have of them? You cannot expect them
to confess this; let them change quietly, no one changes
in public,—be satisfied that they are changed.

"They are as fond of the world as we are; they take up political objects as warmly; they like their own way just as well; they do not like strictness a whit better; they hate spiritual thraldom, and they are half ashamed of the Pope and his Councils. They hardly believe any miracles now, and are annoyed when their own brethren confess that there are such; they never speak of purgatory; they are sore about images; they avoid the subject of Indulgences; and they will not commit themselves to the doctrine of exclusive salvation. The Catholic doctrines are now mere badges of party. Catholics think for themselves and judge for themselves, just as we do; they are kept in their Church by a point of honour, and a reluctance at seeming to abandon a fallen cause."

Such is the judgment of the world, and you are shocked to hear it;—but may it not be that the world knows more about you than you know about yourselves? In proportion as you put off the yoke of Christ, so does the world by a sort of instinct recognize you, and think well of you accordingly. Its highest compliment is to tell you that you disbelieve.

There is an eternal enmity between the world and the Church. Does not the world scoff at all that is glorious, all that is majestic, in our holy religion? Does it not speak against the special creations of God's grace? Does it not disbelieve the possibility of purity and chastity? Does it not slander the profession of celibacy? Does it not deny the virginity of Mary? Does it not cast out her very name as evil? Does it not scorn her as "a dead woman," whom you know to be the Mother of all living, and the great Intercessor of the faithful? Does it not ridicule the Saints? Does it not make light of their relics? Does it not despise the Sacraments? Does it not blaspheme the awful Presence which dwells upon our al-

tars, and mock bitterly and fiercely at our believing that
what it calls bread and wine is that very same Body and
Blood of the Lamb which lay in Mary's womb and hung
on the Cross? What are we, that we should be better
treated than our Lord, and His Mother, and His servants,
and His works? Nay, what are we, if we *be* better treated,
but friends of those who thus treat us well, and who ill-
treat Him? (*D. M. C.*, p. 165ff.)

A SYSTEM of doctrine has risen up during the last three
centuries, in which faith or spiritual-mindedness is contemplated and rested on as the end of religion instead of
Christ. I do not mean to say that Christ is not mentioned as the Author of all good, but that stress is laid
rather on the believing than on the Object of belief, on
the comfort and persuasiveness of the doctrine rather
than on the doctrine itself. And in this way religion is
made to consist in contemplating ourselves, instead of
Christ; not simply in looking to Christ, but in ascer-
taining that we look to Christ, not in His Divinity and
Atonement, but in our conversion and faith in those
truths.

The fashion of the day has been to attempt to convert
by insisting on conversion; to exhort men to undergo
a change; to tell them to be sure they look at Christ,
instead of simply holding up Christ to them; to tell them
to have faith, rather than to supply its Object; to lead
them to stir up and work up their minds, instead of impressing on them the thought of Him who can savingly
work in them; to bid them take care that their faith is
justifying, not dead, formal, self-righteous, or merely
moral, whereas the image of Christ fully delineated of
itself destroys deadness, formality, and self-righteous-

ness; to rely on words, vehemence, eloquence, and the like, rather than to aim at conveying the one great evangelical idea whether in words or not. (*L. J.*, p. 324ff.)

GOD beholds thee individually, whoever thou art. He "calls thee by thy name." He sees thee, and understands thee, as He made thee. He knows what is in thee, all thy own peculiar feelings and thoughts, thy dispositions and likings, thy strength and thy weakness. He views thee in thy day of rejoicing, and thy day of sorrow. He sympathises in thy hopes and thy temptations. He interests Himself in all thy anxieties and remembrances, all the risings and fallings of thy spirit. He has numbered the very hairs of thy head and the cubits of thy stature. He compasses thee round and bears thee in His arms . . . He looks tenderly upon thy hands and thy feet; He hears thy voice, the beating of thy heart, and thy very breathing. Thou dost not love thyself better than He loves thee. Thou canst not shrink from pain more than He dislikes thy bearing it. Thou art chosen to be His, even above thy fellows who dwell in the East and South. What a thought is this—a thought almost too great for our faith! (*P. P. S.*, III. 124f.)

NOTHING is more difficult than to realise that every man has a distinct soul, that every one of all the millions who live or have lived, is as whole and independent a being in himself, as if there were no one else in the whole world but he. To explain what I mean: do you think that the commander of an army realises it when he sends a body of men on some dangerous service? I am not speaking as if he were wrong in so sending them;

I only ask, in matter of fact, does he, think you, commonly understand that each of those poor men has a soul, a soul as dear to himself, as precious in its nature, as his own? Or does he not rather look on the body of men collectively, as one mass, as parts of a whole, as but the wheels or springs of some great machine, to which he assigns the individuality, not to each soul that goes to make it up?

This instance will show what I mean, and how open we all lie to the remark that we do not understand the doctrine of the distinct individuality of the human soul. We class men in masses as we might connect the stones of a building. Consider our common way of regarding history, politics, commerce, and the like, and you will own that I speak truly. We generalise and lay down laws, and then contemplate these creations of our own minds, and act upon and towards them, as if they were the real things, dropping what are more truly such.

Take another instance: when we talk of national greatness, what does it mean? Why, it really means that a certain distinct, definite number of immortal individual beings happen for a few years to be in circumstances to act together and upon one another, in such a way as to be able to act upon the world at large, to gain an ascendancy over the world, to gain power and wealth, and to look like one, and to be talked of and to be looked up to as one. They seem for a short time to be some one thing, and we, from our habit of living by sight, regard them as one, and drop the notion of their being anything else. And when this one dies and that one dies, we forget that it is the passage of separate immortal beings into an unseen state, that the whole which appears is but appearance, and that the component parts are the realities. No, we think nothing of this; but though fresh and fresh men die, and fresh and fresh men are born, so that the whole is ever shifting, yet we forget all that drop away, and are insensible to all that are added; and we still think that this whole which we call the nation is one and the same, and that the individuals that come and go, exist only in it and for it, and are but as the grains of a heap or the leaves of a tree.

Again, survey some populous town: crowds are pouring through the streets, some on foot, some in carriages; while the shops are full and the houses too, could we see into them. Every part of it is full of life. Hence we gain a general idea of splendor, magnificence, opulence, and energy. But what is the truth? Why, that every being in that great concourse is his own centre, and all things about him are but shades, but a "vain shadow," in which he "walketh and disquieteth himself in vain." He has his own hopes and fears, desires, judgments, and aims; he is everything to himself, and no one else is really anything. No one outside of him can really touch him, can touch his soul, his immortality; he must live with himself for ever. He has a depth within him unfathomable, an infinite abyss of existence; and the scene in which he bears part for the moment is but like a gleam of sunshine upon its surface.

Again: when we read history, we meet with accounts of great slaughters and massacres, great pestilences, famines, conflagrations, and so on; and here again we are accustomed in a special way to regard collections of people as if individual units. We cannot understand that a multitude is a collection of immortal souls. All those millions upon millions of human beings who ever trod the earth and saw the sun successively, are at this very moment in existence all together. . . . What a view this sheds upon history! We are accustomed to read it as a tale of fiction, and we forget that it concerns immortal beings! (*P. P. S.* IV. 8off.)

ALL the names we see written on monuments in churches or churchyards, all the writers whose names and works we see in libraries, all the workmen who raised the great buildings, far and near, which are the wonder of the world, they are all in God's remembrance, they all live.

It is the same with those whom we ourselves have seen, who now are departed. I do not now speak of those whom we have known and loved. These we cannot forget, we cannot rid our memory of them; but I speak of all whom we have ever seen; it is also true that they live. Where we know not, but live they do. We may recollect when children, perhaps, once seeing a certain person; and it is almost a dream to us now, that we did. It seems like an accident which goes and all is over, like some creature of the moment, which has no existence beyond it. The rain falls, and the wind blows; and showers and storms have no existence beyond the time when we felt them; they are nothing in themselves. But, if we have once seen any child of Adam, we have seen an immortal soul. It has not passed away as a breeze or sunshine, but it lives; it lives at this moment in one of those many places, whether of bliss or misery, in which all souls are reserved until the end. (*P. P. S.* IV. 85f.)

I REALLY fear, when we come to examine, it will be found there is nothing we resolve, nothing we do, nothing we do not do, nothing we avoid, nothing we choose, nothing we give up, nothing we pursue, which we should not resolve, and do, and not do, and avoid, and choose, and give up, and pursue, if Christ had not died and Heaven were not promised to us. I really fear that most men called Christians, whatever they profess, whatever they may think they feel, whatever warmth and illumination and love they may claim as their own, yet would go on almost as they do, neither much better nor much worse, if they believed Christianity to be a fable. When young they indulge their lusts, or at least pursue the world's vanities; as time goes on they get into a fair way of business, or other mode of making money; then they marry and settle; and, their interest coinciding with their duty, they seem to be, and think themselves, respectable and religious men; they grow attached to things as they are; they begin to have a zeal against vice and error; and they follow after peace with all men.

Such conduct, indeed, as far as it goes, is right and praiseworthy. Only I say it has not necessarily anything to do with religion at all; there is nothing in it which is any proof of the presence of religious principle in those who adopt it; there is nothing they would not do still, though they had nothing to gain from it, except what they gain from it now; they do gain something now, they do gratify their present wishes, they are quiet and orderly because it is their interest and taste to be so; but they venture nothing, they risk, they sacrifice, they abandon nothing on the faith of Christ's word. (*P. P. S.* IV. 301f.)

THE Christian has a deep, silent, hidden peace, which the world sees not—like some well in a retired and shady place, difficult of access. He is the greater part of his time by himself, and when he is in solitude, that is his real state. What he is when left to himself and to his God, that is his true life. He can bear himself; he can (as it were) joy in himself, for it is the grace of God within him, it is the presence of the Eternal Comforter, in which he joys. He can bear, he finds it pleasant, to be with himself at all times—"never less alone than when alone." He can lay his head on his pillow at night, and own in God's sight, with overflowing heart, that he wants nothing,—that he "is full and abounds,"—that God has been all things to him, and that nothing is not his which God could give him. Many hard things may be said of the Christian, and may be done against him, but he has a secret preservative or charm, and minds them not. (*P. P. S.* v. 69f.)

WE BEGIN, by degrees, to perceive that there are but two beings in the whole universe—our own soul, and the God Who made it. Sublime, unlooked-for doctrine, yet most true! To every one of us there are but two beings in the whole world, himself and God. (*P. P. S.* i. 20)

A TRUE Christian may be almost defined as one who has a ruling sense of God's presence within him. (*P. P. S.* v. 225)

BEWARE lest your religion be one of sentiment merely, not of practice. Men may speak in a high imaginative way of the ancient Saints and the Holy Apostolic Church, without making the fervour or refinement of their devotion bear upon their conduct. Many a man likes to be religious in graceful language; he loves religious tales and hymns, yet is never the better Christian for all this. (*P. P. S.* i. 269f.)

MAKE me what *Thou* wouldst have me; I bargain for nothing; I make no terms; I seek for no previous information whither Thou art taking me; I will be what Thou wilt make me, and all that Thou wilt make me. I say not, I will follow Thee withersoever Thou goest, for I am weak; but I give myself to Thee, to lead me anywhither. (*P. P. S.* v. 248)

CAN anything be more marvellous or startling, unless we were used to it, than that we should have a race of beings about us whom we do but see, and as little know their state, or can describe their interests, or their destiny, as we can tell of the inhabitants of the sun and moon? It is indeed a very overpowering thought, when we get to fix our minds on it, that we familiarly use, I may say hold intercourse with, creatures who are as much strangers to us, as mysterious, as if they were the fabulous, unearthly beings, more powerful than man, and yet his slaves, which Eastern superstitions have invented. They have apparently passions, habits, and a certain accountableness, but all is mystery about them. We do not know whether they can sin or not, whether they are under punishment, whether they are to live after this life. Is it not plain to our senses that there is a world inferior to us in the scale of beings, with which we are connected without understanding what it is? And is it difficult to faith to admit the word of Scripture concerning our connection with a world superior to us? (*P. P. S.* IV. 205f.)

NATURE is not inanimate; its daily toil is intelligent; its works are *duties*. (*P. P. S.* II. 361)

WHENEVER we look abroad, we are reminded of those most gracious and holy Beings, the servants of the Holiest, who deign to minister to the heirs of salvation. Every breath of air and ray of light and heat, every beautiful prospect, is, as it were, the skirts of their garments, the waving of the robes of those whose faces see God in Heaven. (*P. P. S.* II. 362)

HOW much has every herb and flower in it to surprise and overwhelm us! For, even did we know as much about them as the wisest of men, yet there are those around us, though unseen, to whom our greatest knowledge is as ignorance; and, when we converse on subjects of nature scientifically, repeating the names of plants and earths, and describing their properties, we should do so religiously, as in the hearing of the great servants of God, with the sort of diffidence that we always feel in speaking before the learned and wise of our own mortal race, as poor beginners in intellectual knowledge, as well as in moral attainments. (*P. P. S.* II. 365)

THE world seems to go on as usual. There is nothing of heaven in the face of society; in the news of the day there is nothing of heaven; in the faces of the many, of the great, or of the rich, or of the busy, there is nothing of heaven; in the words of the eloquent, or the deeds of the powerful, or the counsels of the wise, or the resolves of the lordly, or the pomps of the wealthy, there is nothing of heaven. And yet the ever-blessed Spirit of God is here; the presence of the eternal Son, ten times more glorious, more powerful than when He trod the earth in our flesh, is with us. Let us ever bear in mind this Divine truth: the more secret God's hand is, the more powerful—the more silent, the more awful. (*P. P. S.* IV. 265)

IF BEAUTIFULNESS is all that is needed to make a thing right, then nothing graceful and pleasant can be wrong; and, since there is no abstract idea but admits of being embellished and dressed up, and made pleasant and graceful, it follows as a matter of course that any thing whatever is permissible. One sees at once, that, taking men as they are, the love of the Beautiful will be nothing short of the love of the Sensual. (*H. S.* III. 84f.)

LIBERALISM in religion is the doctrine that there is no positive truth in religion, but that one creed is as good as another, and this is the teaching which is gaining substance and force daily. It is inconsistent with any recognition of any religion, as *true*. It teaches that all are to be tolerated, for all are matters of opinion. Revealed religion is not a truth, but a sentiment and a taste; not an objective fact, not miraculous; and it is the right of each individual to make it say just what strikes his fancy. Devotion is not necessarily founded on faith. Men may go to Protestant Churches and to Catholic, may get good from both and belong to neither. They may fraternize together in spiritual thoughts and feelings, without having any views at all of doctrines in common, or seeing the need of them. Since, then, religion is so personal a peculiarity and so private a possession, we must of necessity ignore it in the intercourse of man with man. If a man puts on a new religion every morning, what is that to you? It is as impertinent to think about a man's religion as about his sources of income, or his management of his family. Religion is in no sense the bond of society. . . .

Hitherto it has been considered that religion alone, with its supernatural sanctions, was strong enough to secure submission of the masses of our population to law and order; now the philosophers and politicians are bent on satisfying this problem without the aid of Christianity. Instead of the Church's authority and teaching, they would substitute first of all a universal and thoroughly secular education, calculated to bring home to every individual that to be orderly, industrious, and sober is his personal interest. Then, for great working principles to take the place of religion, for the use of the masses thus carefully educated, it provides the broad, fundamental, ethical truths of justice, benevolence, veracity, and the like; proved experience; and those natural laws which exist and act spontaneously in society, and in social matters, whether physical or psychological; for instance, in government, trade, finance, sanitary experiments, and the intercourse of nations. As to Religion, it is a private luxury, which a man may have if he will; but which, of course, he must pay for, and which he must not obtrude upon others, or indulge in to their annoyance.

The general nature of this great *apostasia* is one and the same everywhere; but in detail, and in character, it varies in different countries. For myself, I would rather speak of it in my own country, which I know. There, I think it threatens to have a formidable success; though it is not easy to see what will be its ultimate issue. At first sight it might be thought that Englishmen are too religious for a movement which, on the Continent, seems to be founded on infidelity; but the misfortune with us is that, though it ends in infidelity as in other places, it does not necessarily arise out of infidelity. It must be recollected that the religious sects, which sprang up in England three centuries ago, and which are so powerful now, have ever been fiercely opposed to the Union of Church and State, and would advocate the un-Christianizing of the monarchy and all that belongs to it, under the notion that such a catastrophe would make Christianity much more pure and much more powerful.

Next, the Liberal principle is forced on us from the necessity of the case. Consider what follows from the very fact of these many sects. They constitute the religion, it is supposed, of half the population; and, recollect, our mode of government is popular. Every dozen men taken at random whom you meet in the streets have a share in political power; when you inquire into their forms of belief, perhaps they represent one or other of as many as seven religions; how can they possibly act together in municipal or in national matters, if each insists on the recognition of his own religious denomination? All action would be at a deadlock unless the subject of religion were ignored. We cannot help ourselves.

And, thirdly, it must be borne in mind that there is much in the liberalistic theory which is good and true; for example, not to say more, the precepts of justice, truthfulness, sobriety, self-command, benevolence, which, as I have already noted, are among its avowed principles, and the natural laws of society. It is not till we find that this array of principles is intended to supersede, to block out, religion, that we pronounce it to be evil. There never was a device of the Enemy so cleverly framed and with such promise of success. And already it has answered to the expectations which have been formed of it. It is sweeping into its own ranks great numbers of able, earnest, virtuous men, elderly men of approved antecedents, young men with a career before them.

Such is the state of things in England, and it is well that it should be realized by all of us; but it must not be supposed for a moment that I am afraid of it. I lament it deeply, because I foresee that it may be the ruin of many souls; but I have no fear at all that it really can do aught of serious harm to the Word of God, to Holy Church, to our Almighty King, the Lion of the tribe of Judah, Faithful and True, or to His Vicar on earth. Christianity has been too often in what seemed deadly peril that we should fear for it any new trial now. So far is certain; on the other hand, what is uncertain, and in these great contests commonly is uncertain, and what is commonly a great surprise, when it is witnessed, is the particular mode by which, in the event, Providence rescues and saves His elect inheritance. Sometimes our enemy is turned into a friend; sometimes he is despoiled of that special virulence of evil which was so threatening; sometimes he falls to pieces himself; sometimes he does just so much as is beneficial, and then is removed. Commonly the Church has nothing more to do than to go on in her own proper duties, in confidence and peace; to stand still and to see the salvation of God. (*Ward* II. 46off.*)

TURN away from the Catholic Church, and to whom will you go? it is your only chance of peace and assurance in this turbulent, changing world. There is nothing between it and scepticism, when men exert their reason freely. Private creeds, fancy religions, may be showy

* From Newman's address in Rome on being made Cardinal.

and imposing to the many in their day; national religions may lie huge and lifeless, and cumber the ground for centuries, and distract the attention or confuse the judgment of the learned; but on the long run it will be found that either the Catholic Religion is verily and indeed the coming in of the unseen world into this, or that there is nothing positive, nothing dogmatic, nothing real in any of our notions as to whence we come and whither we are going. . . .

Oh, perverse children of men, who refuse truth when offered you, because it is not truer! Oh, restless hearts and fastidious intellects, who seek a gospel more salutary than the Redeemer's and a creation more perfect than the Creator's! God, forsooth, is not great enough for you; you have those high aspirations and those philosophical notions, inspired by the original Tempter, which are content with nothing that is, which determine that the Most High is too little for your worship, and His attributes too narrow for your love. (*D. M. C.*, p. 282f.)

GIBBON has mentioned five causes in explanation of [the rise and establishment of Christianity], viz. the zeal of Christians, inherited from the Jews; their doctrine of a future state; their claim to miraculous power; their virtues; and their ecclesiastical organization. Let us briefly consider them.

He thinks these five causes, when combined, will fairly account for the event; but he has not thought of accounting for their combination. If they are ever so available for his purpose, still that availableness arises out of their coincidence, and out of what does that coincidence arise? Until this is explained, nothing is explained, and the question had better have been let alone. These presumed causes are quite distinct from each other, and, I say, the wonder is, what made them come together. How came a multitude of Gentiles to be influenced with Jewish zeal? How came zealots to submit to a strict, ecclesiastical *régime?* What connexion has such a *régime* with the immortality of the soul? Why should immortality, a philosophical doctrine, lead to belief in miracles, which is a superstition of the vulgar? What tendency had miracles and magic to make men austerely virtuous? Lastly, what power had a code of virtue, as calm and enlightened as that of Antoninus, to generate a zeal as fierce as that of Maccabæus? Wonderful events before now have apparently been nothing but coincidences, certainly; but they do not become less wonderful by cataloguing their constituent causes, unless we also show how these came to be constituent.

However, this by the way; the real question is this . . . are these historical characteristics of Christianity, also in matter of fact, historical causes of Christianity? Has Gibbon given proof that they are? Has he brought evidence of their operation, or does he simply conjecture in his private judgment that they operated? Whether they were adapted to accomplish a certain work, is a matter of opinion; whether they did accomplish it is a question of fact. He ought to adduce instances of their efficiency before he has a right to say that they are efficient. And the second question is, what is this effect, of which they are to be considered as causes? It is no other than this, the conversion of bodies of men to the Christian faith. Let us keep this in view. We have to determine whether these five characteristics of Christianity were efficient causes of bodies of men becoming Christians. I think they neither did effect such conversions, nor were adapted to do so, and for these reasons:

1. For first, as to zeal, by which Gibbon means party spirit, or *esprit de corps;* this doubtless is a motive principle when men are already members of a body, but does it operate in bringing them into it? The Jews were born in Judaism, they had a long and glorious history, and would naturally feel and show *esprit de corps;* but how did party spirit tend to bring Jew or Gentile out of his own place into a new society, and that a society which as yet scarcely was formed into a society? Zeal, certainly, may be felt for a cause, or for a person; on this point I shall speak presently; but Gibbon's idea of Christian zeal is nothing better than the old wine of Judaism decanted into new Christian bottles, and would be too flat a stimulant, even if it admitted of such a transference, to be taken as a cause of conversion to Christianity without definite evidence, in proof of the fact. Christians had zeal for Christianity after they were converted, not before.

2. Next, as to the doctrine of a future state. Gibbon seems to mean by this doctrine the fear of hell; now certainly in this day there are persons converted from sin to a religious life by vivid descriptions of the future punishment of the wicked; but then it must be recollected that such persons already believe in the doctrine thus urged upon them. On the contrary, give some tract upon hell-fire to one of the wild boys in a large town, who has had no education, has no faith; and, instead of being startled by it, he will laugh at it as something frightfully ridiculous. The belief in Styx and Tartarus was dying out of the world at the time that Christianity came, as the parallel belief now seems to be dying out in all classes of our own society. The doctrine of eternal punishment does only anger the multitude of men in our large towns now, and make them blaspheme; why should

it have had any other effect on the heathen populations in the age when our Lord came? Yet it was among those populations that He and His made their way from the first. As to the hope of eternal life, that doubtless, as well as the fear of hell, was a most operative doctrine in the case of men who had been actually converted, of Christians brought before the magistrate, or writhing under torture; but the thought of eternal glory does not keep bad men from a bad life now, and why should it convert them then from their pleasant sins, to a heavy, mortified, joyless existence, to a life of ill-usage, fright, contempt, and desolation?

3. That the claim to miracles should have any wide influence in favour of Christianity among heathen populations, who had plenty of portents of their own, is an opinion in curious contrast with the objection against Christianity which has provoked an answer from Paley, viz. that "Christian miracles are not recited or appealed to, by early Christian writers themselves, so fully or so frequently as might have been expected." Paley solves the difficulty as far as it is a fact, by observing, as I have suggested, that "it was their lot to contend with magical agency, against which the mere production of these facts was not sufficient for the convincing of their adversaries." "I do not know," he continues, "whether they themselves thought it quite decisive of the controversy." A claim to miraculous power on the part of Christians, which is so infrequent as to become an objection to the fact of their possessing it, can hardly have been a principal cause of their success.

4. And how is it possible to imagine with Gibbon that what he calls the "sober and domestic virtues" of Christians, their "aversion to the luxury of the age," their "chastity, temperance, and economy," that these dull

qualities were persuasives of a nature to win and melt the hard heathen heart, in spite too of the dreary prospect of the *barathrum*, the amphitheatre, and the stake? Did the Christian morality by its severe beauty make a convert of Gibbon himself? On the contrary, he bitterly says, "It was not in this world that the primitive Christians were desirous of making themselves either agreeable or useful." "The virtue of the primitive Christians, like that of the first Romans, was very frequently guarded by poverty and ignorance." "Their gloomy and austere aspect, their abhorrence of the common business and pleasures of life, and their frequent predictions of impending calamities, inspired the Pagans with the apprehension of some danger which would arise from the new sect." Here we have not only Gibbon hating their moral and social bearing, but his heathen also. How then were those heathen overcome by the amiableness of that which they viewed with such disgust? We have here plain proof that the Christian character repelled the heathen; where is the evidence that it converted them?

5. Lastly, as to the ecclesiastical organization, this, doubtless, as time went on, was a special characteristic of the new religion; but how could it directly contribute to its extension? Of course it gave it strength, but it did not give it life. We are not born of bones and muscles. It is one thing to make conquests, another to consolidate an empire. Before Constantine, Christians made their great conquests. Rules are for settled times, not for time of war.

I do not deny that Gibbon's Five Causes might have operated now and then; but Christianity made its way, not by individual, but by broad, wholesale conversions, and the question is, how they originated?

It is very remarkable that it should not have occurred

to a man of Gibbon's sagacity to enquire, what account
the Christians themselves gave of the matter. Would it
not have been worth while for him to have let conjecture alone, and to have looked for facts instead? Why
did he not try the hypothesis of faith, hope, and charity?
Did he never hear of love towards God, and faith in
Christ? Did he not recollect the many words of Apostles, Bishops, Apologists, Martyrs, all forming one testimony? No; such thoughts are close upon him, and
close upon the truth; but he cannot sympathize with
them, he cannot believe in them, he cannot even enter
into them, *because* he needs the due preparation of mind.
(*G. of A.*, p. 457ff.)

THE essence of Religion is the idea of a Moral Governor and a particular Providence. (*D. and A.*, p. 303)

I AM tempted to try whether a monster indictment,
similarly frightful and similarly fantastical to that which
is got up against Catholicism, might not be framed
against some other institution or power, of parallel greatness and excellence to the communion of Rome. For this
purpose I will take the British Constitution, which is so
specially the possession and the glory of our own people;
I would show you how even it, the British Constitution,
would fare, when submitted to the intellect of Exeter
Hall, and handled by practitioners, whose highest effort
at dissection is to chop and to mangle.

I will suppose, then, a speaker, and an audience too,
who never saw England, never saw a member of parliament, a policeman, a queen, or a London mob; who never
read the English history, nor studied any one of our phi-

losophers, jurists, moralists, or poets; but who has dipped
into Blackstone and several English writers, and has
picked up facts at third or fourth hand, and has got together a crude farrago of ideas, words, and instances, a
little truth, a deal of falsehood, a deal of misrepresenta-
tion, a deal of nonsense, and a deal of invention. And
most fortunately for my purpose, here is an account
transmitted express by the private correspondent of a
morning paper, of a great meeting held about a fortnight
since at Moscow, under sanction of the Czar, on occasion
of an attempt made by one or two Russian noblemen to
spread British ideas in his capital. It seems the emperor
thought it best in the present state of men's minds, when
secret societies are so rife, to put down the movement by
argument rather than by a military force; and so he instructed the governor of Moscow to connive at the
project of a great public meeting which should be opened
to the small faction of Anglomaniacs, or John-Bullists, as
they are popularly termed, as well as to the mass of the
population. As many as ten thousand men, as far as the
writer could calculate, were gathered together in one of
the largest *places* of the city; a number of spirited and
impressive speeches were made; but the most successful
of all is said to have been the final harangue, by a member of a junior branch of the Potemkin family, once one
of the imperial aides-de-camp, who has spent the last
thirty years in the wars of the Caucasus. This distinguished veteran, who has acquired the title of Blood-
sucker, from his extraordinary gallantry in combat with
the Circassian tribes, spoke at great length; and the express contains a portion of his highly inflammatory address, of which, and of certain consequences which followed it, the British minister is said already to have
asked an explanation of the cabinet of St. Petersburg: I

transcribe it as it may be supposed to stand in the morning print:

The Count began by observing that the events of every day, as it came, called on his countrymen more and more importunately to choose their side, and to make a firm stand against a perfidious power, which arrogantly proclaims that there is nothing like the British Constitution in the whole world, and that no country can prosper without it; which is yearly aggrandizing itself in East, West, and South, which is engaged in one enormous conspiracy against all States, and which was even aiming at modifying the old institutions of the North, and at dressing up the army, navy, legislature, and executive of his own country in the livery of Queen Victoria. "Insular in situation," he exclaimed, "and at the back gate of the world, what has John Bull to do with continental matters, or with the political traditions of our holy Russia?" And yet there were men in that very city who were so far the dupes of insidious propagandists and insolent traitors to their emperor, as to maintain that England had been a civilized country longer than Russia. On the contrary, he maintained, and he would shed the last drop of his blood in maintaining, that, as for its boasted Constitution, it was a crazy, old-fashioned piece of furniture, and an eyesore in the nineteenth century, and would not last a dozen years. He had the best information for saying so. He could understand those who had never crossed out of their island, listening to the songs about "Rule Britannia," and "*Rosbif*," and "Poor Jack," and the "Old English Gentleman"; he understood and he pitied them; but that Russians, that the conquerors of Napoleon, that the heirs of a paternal government, should bow the knee, and kiss the hand, and walk backwards, and perform other antics before the face of a limited monarch, this was the incomprehensible foolery which certain Russians had viewed with so much tenderness. He repeated, there were in that city educated men, who had openly professed a reverence for the atheistical tenets and fiendish maxims of John-Bullism.

Here the speaker was interrupted by one or two murmurs of dissent, and a foreigner, supposed to be a partner in a Scotch firm, was observed in the extremity of the square, making earnest attempts to obtain a hearing. He was put down, however, amid enthusiastic cheering, and the Count proceeded with a warmth of feeling which increased the effect of the terrible invective which followed. He said he had used the words "atheistical" and "fiendish" most advisedly, and he would give his reasons for doing so. What was to be said to any political power which claimed the attribute of Divinity? Was any term too strong for such a usurpation? Now, no one would deny Antichrist would be such a power: an Antichrist was contemplated, was predicted in Scripture, it was to come in the last times, it was to grow slowly, it was to manifest itself warily and craftily, and then to have a mouth speaking great things against the Divinity and against His attributes. This prediction was most literally and exactly fulfilled in the British Constitution. Antichrist was not only to usurp, but to profess to usurp the arms of heaven—he was to arrogate its titles. This was the special mark of the beast, and where was it fulfilled but in John-Bullism? "I hold in my hand," continued the speaker, "a book which I have obtained under very remarkable circumstances. It is not known to the British people, it is circulated only among the lawyers, merchants, and aristocracy, and its restrictive use is secured only by the most solemn oaths, the most fearful penalties, and the utmost vigilance of the police. I procured it after many years of anxious search by the activity of an agent, and the coöperation of an English bookseller, and it cost me an enormous sum to make it my own. It is called *Blackstone's Commentaries on the Laws of England*, and I am happy to make known to the universe its odious and shocking mysteries, known to few Britons, and certainly not known to the deluded persons whose vagaries have been the occasion of this meeting. I am sanguine in thinking that when they come to know the real tenets of John Bull, they will at once disown his doctrines with horror, and break off all connection with his adherents.

"Now, I should say, gentlemen, that this book, while it is confined to certain classes, is of those classes, on the other hand, of judges, and lawyers, and privy councilors, and justices of the peace, and police magistrates, and clergy, and country gentlemen, the guide, and I may say, the gospel. I open the book, gentlemen, and what are the first words which meet my eyes? '*The King can do no wrong.*' I beg you to attend, gentlemen, to this most significant assertion; one was accustomed to think that no child of man had the gift of impeccability; one had imagined that, simply speaking, impeccability was a divine attribute; but this British Bible, as I may call it, distinctly ascribes an absolute sinlessness to the King of Great Britain and Ireland. Observe, I am using no words of my own, I am still but quoting what meets my eyes in this remarkable document. The words run thus: 'It is an axiom of the law of the land that the *King himself can do no wrong.*' Was I wrong, then, in speaking of the atheistical maxims of John-Bullism? But this is far from all: the writer goes on actually to ascribe to the Sovereign (I tremble while I pronounce the words) *absolute perfection;* for he speaks thus: 'The law ascribes to the King in his political capacity ABSOLUTE PERFECTION; the *King can do no wrong!'*—(groans). One had thought that no human power could thus be described; but the British legislature, judicature, and jurisprudence, have had the unspeakable effrontery to impute to their crowned and sceptered idol, to their "doll,"—here cries of "shame, shame," from the same individual who had distinguished himself in an earlier part of the speech—"to this doll, this puppet whom they have dressed up with a lion and a unicorn, the attribute of ABSOLUTE PERFECTION!" Here the individual who had several times interrupted the speaker sprang up, in spite of the efforts of persons about him to keep him down, and cried out, as far as his words could be collected, "You cowardly liar, our dear good little Queen," when he was immediately saluted with a cry of "Turn him out," and soon made his exit from the meeting.

Order being restored, the Count continued: "Gentlemen, I could wish you would have suffered this emissary of a foreign potentate (immense cheering), who is insidiously aiming at forming a political party among us, to have heard to the end that black catalogue of charges against his Sovereign, which as yet I have barely commenced. Gentlemen, I was saying that the Queen of England challenges the divine attribute of ABSOLUTE PERFECTION! but, as if this were not enough this Blackstone continues, 'The King, moreover, is not incapable of *doing* wrong, but even of *thinking* wrong!! *he can never do an improper thing; in him is no* FOLLY *or* WEAKNESS!!!'" (Shudders and cheers from the vast assemblage, which lasted alternately some minutes.) At the same time a respectably dressed gentleman below the platform begged permission to look at the book; it was immediately handed to him; after looking at the passages, he was observed to inspect carefully the title-page and binding; he then returned it without a word.

The Count, in resuming his speech, observed that he courted and challenged investigation, he should be happy to answer any question, and he hoped soon to publish, by subscription, a translation of the work, from which he had been quoting. Then, resuming the subject where he had left it, he made some most forcible and impressive reflections on the miserable state of those multitudes, who, in spite of their skill in the mechanical arts, and their political energy, were in the leading-strings of so foul a superstition. The passage he had quoted was the first and mildest of a series of blasphemies so prodigious, that he really feared to proceed, not only from disgust at the necessity of uttering them, but lest he should be taxing the faith of his hearers beyond what appeared reasonable limits. Next, then, he drew attention to the point that the English Sovereign distinctly claimed, according to the same infamous work, to be the "*fount* of justice"; and, that there might be no mistake in the matter, the author declared, "that she *is never bound in justice to do anything.*" What, then, is her method of acting? Unwilling as he was to defile his lips with so profane a statement, he must tell them that this abominable writer coolly declared that the Queen, a woman, only did acts of reparation and restitution as a matter of *grace*! He was not a theologian, he had spent his life in the field, but he knew enough of his religion to be able to say that grace was a word especially proper to the appointment and decrees of Divine Sovereignty. All his hearers knew perfectly well that nature was one thing, grace another; and yet here was a poor child of clay claiming to be the fount, not only of justice, but of grace. She was making herself a first cause of not merely natural, but spiritual excellence, and doing nothing more or less than simply emancipating herself from her Maker. The Queen, it seemed, never obeyed the law of compulsion, according to Blackstone; that is, her Maker could not compel her. This was no mere deduction of his own, as directly would be seen. Let it be observed, the Apostle called the predicted Antichrist "the wicked one," or, as it might be more correctly translated, "the lawless," because he was to be the proud despiser of all law; now, wonderful to say, this was the very assumption of the British Parliament. "The Power of Parliament," said Sir Edward Coke, "is so transcendent and absolute, that it cannot be *confined* within any bounds!! It has sovereign and uncontrollable authority!!" Moreover, the Judges had declared that "it is so high and mighty in its nature, that it *may make law*, and THAT WHICH IS LAW IT MAY MAKE NO LAW!" Here verily was the mouth speaking great things; but there was more behind, which, but for the atrocious sentiments he had already admitted into his mouth, he really should not have the courage, the endurance to utter. It was sickening to the soul, and intellect, and feelings of a Russ, to form the words on his tongue, and the ideas in his imagination. He would say what must be said as quickly as he could, and without comment. The gallant speaker then delivered the following passage from Blackstone's volume, in a very distinct and articulate whisper: "Some have not scrupled to call its power—the OMNIPOTENCE of Parliament!" No one can conceive the thrilling effect of these words; they were heard all over the immense assemblage; every man turned pale; a dead silence followed; one might have heard a pin drop. A pause of some minutes followed.

The speaker continued, evidently laboring under intense emotion:—"Have you not heard enough, my dear compatriots, of this hideous system of John-Bullism? was I wrong in using the words fiendish and atheistical when I entered upon this subject? and need I proceed further with blasphemous details, which cannot really add to the monstrous bearing of the passages I have already read to you? If the Queen 'cannot do wrong,' if she 'cannot even think wrong,' if she is 'absolute perfection,' if she has 'no folly, no weakness,' if she is the 'fount of justice,' if she is 'the fount of grace,' if she is simply 'above law,' if she is 'omnipotent,' what wonder that the lawyers of John-Bullism should also call her 'sacred!' what wonder that they should speak of her as 'majesty!' what wonder that they should speak of her as a 'superior being!' Here again I am using the words of the book I hold in my hand. 'The people' (my blood runs cold while I repeat them) 'are led to consider their Sovereign *in the light of a* SUPERIOR BE-ING.' 'Every one is under him,' says Bracton, 'and he is under no one.' Accordingly, the law books call his *Vicarious Dei in terra*, 'the Vicar of God on earth'; a most astonishing fulfillment, you observe, of the prophecy for Antichrist is a Greek word, which means 'Vicar of Christ.' What wonder, under these circumstances, that Queen Elizabeth, assuming the attribute of the Creator, once said to one of her Bishops: 'Proud Prelate, *I made you, and I can unmake you!*' What wonder that James the First had the brazen assurance to say, that 'As it is atheism and blasphemy in a creature to dispute the Deity, so it is presumption and sedition in a subject to dispute a King in the height of his power!' Moreover, his subjects called him the 'breath of their nostrils'; and my Lord Clarendon, the present Lord Lieutenant of Ireland, in his celebrated *History of the Rebellion*, declares that the same haughty monarch actually on one occasion called himself 'a God'; and in his great legal digest, commonly called the 'Constitutions of Clarendon,' he gives us the whole account of the King's banishing the Archbishop, St. Thomas of Canterbury, for refusing to do him homage. Lord Bacon, too, went nearly as far when he called him *Deaster quidam*, 'some sort of little god.' Alexander Pope, too, calls Queen Anne a goddess: and Addison, with a servility only equalled by his profaneness, cries out, 'Thee, goddess, thee Britannia's isle adores.' Nay, even at this very time, when public attention has been drawn to the subject, Queen Victoria causes herself to be represented on her coins as the goddess of the seas, with a pagan trident in her hand.

"Gentlemen, can it surprise you to be told, after such an exposition of the blasphemies of England, that, astonishing to say, Queen Victoria is distinctly pointed out in the Book of Revelation as having the number of the beast! You may recollect that number is 666; now, she came to the throne in the year thirty-seven, at which date she was eighteen years old. Multiply then 37 by 18, and you have the very number 666, which is the mystical emblem of the lawless King!!!

"No wonder then, with such monstrous pretensions, and such awful auguries, that John-Bullism is, in act and deed, as savage and profligate as in profession it is saintly and innocent. Its annals are marked with blood and corruption. The historian Hallam, though one of the ultrabullist party, in his *Constitutional History*, admits that the English tribunals are 'disgraced by the brutal manners and iniquitous partiality of the bench.' 'The general behavior of the bench,' he says elsewhere, 'has covered it with infamy.' Soon after, he tells us that the dominant faction inflicted on the High Church Clergy 'the disgrace and remorse of perjury.' The English Kings have been the curse and shame of human nature. Richard the First boasted that the evil spirit was the father of his family; of Henry the Second St. Bernard said, 'From the devil he came, and to the devil he will go'; William the Second was killed by the enemy of man, to whom he had sold himself, while hunting in one of his forests; Henry the First died of eating lampreys; John died of eating peaches; Clarence, a king's brother, was drowned in a butt of malmsey wine; Richard the Third put to death his Sovereign, his Sovereign's son, his two brothers, his wife, two nephews, and half-a-dozen friends. Henry the Eighth successively married and murdered no less than six hundred women. I quote the words of the *Edinburgh Review*, that, according to Hollinshed, no less than 70,000 persons died under the hand of the executioner in his reign. Sir John Fortescue tells us that in his day there were more persons executed for robbery in England in one year, than in France in seven. Four hundred persons a year were executed in the reign of Queen Elizabeth. Even so late as the last century, in spite of the continued protests of foreign nations, in the course of seven years there were 428 capital convictions in London alone. Burning of children, too, is a favorite punishment with John Bull, as may be seen in this same Blackstone, who notices the burning of a girl of thirteen given by Sir Matthew Hale. The valets always assassinate their masters; lovers uniformly strangle their sweethearts; the farmers and the farmers' wives universally beat their apprentices to death; and their lawyers in the inns of court strip and starve their servants, as has appeared from remarkable investigations in the law courts during the last year. Husbands sell their wives by public auction with a rope round their necks. An intelligent Frenchman, M. Pellet, who visited London in 1815, deposes that he saw a number of skulls on each side of the river Thames, and he was told they were found especially thick at the landing-places among the watermen. But why multiply instances, when the names of those two-legged tigers, Rush, Thistlewood, Thurtell, the Mannings, Colonel Kirk, Claverhouse, Simon de Monteforte, Strafford, the Duke of Cumberland, Warren Hastings, and Judge Jeffreys, are household words all over the earth? John-Bullism, through a space of 800 years, is *semper idem,* unchangeable in evil. One hundred and sixty offenses are punishable with death. It is death to live with gypsies for a month; and Lord Hale mentions thirteen persons as having, in his day, suffered death thereon at one assize. It is death to steal a sheep, death to rob a warren, death to steal a letter, death to steal a handkerchief, death to cut down a cherry tree. And, after all, the excesses of John-Bullism at home are mere child's play to the oceans of blood it has shed abroad. It has been the origin of all the wars which have desolated Europe; it has fomented national jealousy, and the antipathy of castes in every part of the world; it has plunged flourishing states into the abyss of revolution. The Crusades, the Sicilian Vespers, the wars of the Reformation, the Thirty Years' War, the War of Succession, the Seven Years' War, the American War, the French Revolution, all are simply owing to John-Bull ideas; and to take one definite instance, in the course of the last war, the deaths of two millions of the human race lie at his door; for the Whigs themselves, from first to last, and down to this day, admit and proclaim, without any hesitation or limitation, that that war was simply and entirely the work of John-Bullism, and needed not, and would not have been, but for its influence, and its alone.

"Such is that 'absolute perfection, without folly and without weakness,' which, reveling in the blood of man, is still seeking out her victims, and scenting blood all over the earth. It is that woman Jezebel, who fulfills the prophetic vision, and incurs the prophetic denunciation. And, strange to say, a prophet of her own has not scrupled to

apply to her that very appellation. Dead to good and evil,
the children of Jezebel glory in the name; and ten years
have not passed since, by a sort of infatuation, one of the
very highest Tories in the land, a minister, too, of the
established religion, hailed the bloodstained Monarchy
under the very title of the mystical sorceress. Jezebel
surely is her name, and Jezebel is her nature; for drunk
with the spiritual wine cup of wrath, and given over to
believe a lie, at length she has ascended to heights which
savor rather of madness than of pride; she babbles absurdities, and she thirsts for impossibilities. Gentlemen,
I am speaking the words of sober seriousness; I can prove
what I say to the letter; the extravagance is not in me
but in the object of my denunciation. Once more I appeal
to the awful volume I hold in my hands. I appeal to it, I
open it, I cast it from me. Listen, then, once again; it is
a fact; Jezebel has declared her own *omnipresence*. 'A
consequence of the royal prerogatives,' says the anti-
christian author, 'is the legal UBIQUITY of the King!' 'His
Majesty is always *present* in all his courts: his judges are
the *mirror* by which the King's image is reflected'; and
further, 'From this *ubiquity*' (you see he is far from
shrinking from the word), 'from this *ubiquity* it follows
that the Sovereign can never be NONSUIT!!' Gentlemen,
the sun would set before I told you one hundredth part
of the enormity of this child of Moloch and Belial. In-
ebriated with the cup of insanity, and flung upon the
stream of recklessness, she dashes down the cataract of
nonsense, and whirls amid the pools of confusion. Like
the Roman emperor, she actually has declared herself
immortal! she has declared her eternity! Again, I am
obliged to say it, these are no words of mine; the tremendous sentiment confronts me in black and crimson
characters in this diabolical book. 'In the law,' says Black-

stone, 'the Sovereign is said *never to die!*' Again, with still more hideous expressiveness, 'The law ascribes to the Sovereign an ABSOLUTE IMMORTALITY. THE KING NEVER DIES.'

"And now, gentlemen, your destiny is in your own hands. If you are willing to succumb to a power which has never been contented with what she was, but has been for centuries extending her conquests in both hemispheres, then the humble individual who has addressed you will submit to the necessary consequence; will resume his military dress, and return to the Caucasus; but if, on the other hand, as I believe, you are resolved to resist unflinchingly this flood of satanical imposture and foul ambition, and force it back into the ocean; if, not from hatred to the English—far from it—from *love* to them (for a distinction must ever be drawn between the nation and its dominant John-Bullism); if, I say, from love to them as brothers, from a generous determination to fight their battles, from an intimate consciousness that they are in their secret hearts *Russians,* that they are champing the bit of their iron lot, and are longing for you as their deliverers; if, from these lofty notions as well as from a burning patriotism, you will form the high resolve to annihilate this dishonor of humanity; if you loathe its sophisms, *De minimis non curat lex,* and *Malitia supplet ætatem,* and *Tres faciunt collegium,* and *Impotentia excusat legem,* and 'Possession is nine parts of the law,' and 'The greater the truth, the greater the libel' —principles which sap the very foundations of morals; if you wage war to the knife with its blighting superstitions of primogeniture, gavelkind, mortmain, and contingent reminders; if you detest, abhor, and adjure the tortuous maxims and perfidious provisions of its *habeas corpus, quare impedit,* and *qui tam* (hear, hear); if you scorn the mummeries of its wigs and bands, and coifs, and ermine (vehement cheering); if you trample and spit upon its accursed fee simple and fee tail, villanage, and free soccage, fiefs, heriots, seizins, feuds (a burst of cheers, the whole meeting in commotion); its shares, its premiums, its post-obits, its percentages, its tariffs, its broad and narrow gauge"—Here the cheers became frantic, and drowned the speaker's voice, and a most extraordinary scene of enthusiasm followed. One half of the meeting was seen embracing the other half; till, as if by the force of a sudden resolution, they all poured out of the square, and proceeded to break the windows of all the British residents. They then formed into procession, and directing their course to the great square before the Kremlin, they dragged through the mud, and then solemnly burned, an effigy of John Bull which had been provided beforehand by the managing committee, a lion and unicorn, and a Queen Victoria. These being fully consumed, they dispersed quietly; and by ten o'clock at night the streets were profoundly still, and the silver moon looked down in untroubled lustre on the city of the Czars.

Now I protest my full conviction that I have not caricatured this parallel at all. Were I, indeed, skilled in legal matters, I could have made it far more natural, plausible, and complete; but, as for its extravagance, I say deliberately, and have means of knowing what I say, having once been a Protestant, and being now a Catholic—knowing what is said and thought of Catholics, on the one hand, and, on the other, knowing what they really *are*— I deliberately assert that no absurdities contained in the above sketch can equal—nay, that no conceivable absurdities can surpass—the absurdities which are firmly believed of Catholics by sensible, kind-hearted, well-intentioned Protestants. Such is the consequence of having looked at things all on one side, and shutting the eyes to the other.

(*P. P. C.*, p. 25ff.)

[I WAS confirmed] in my distrust of the reality of material phenomena, and [made to] rest in the thought of two and two only supreme and luminously self-evident beings, myself and my creator. (*Apol.*, p. 108.)

THE misery for me, which would have been, had I not followed on, had I hung back [from Catholicism] when Christ called! Oh, the utter confusion of mind, the wreck of faith and opinion, the blackness and void, the dreary scepticism, the hopelessness which would have been my lot, the pledge of the outer darkness to come, had I been afraid to follow Him! I have lost friends, I have lost the world, but I have gained Him, who gives in Himself houses and brethren and sisters and mothers and children and lands a hundred-fold; I have lost the perishable, and gained the Infinite; I have lost time, and I have gained eternity. (*D. M. C.*, p. 236f.)

MAY He, as of old, choose "the foolish things of the world to confound the wise, and the weak things of the world to confound the things which are mighty!" May He support us all the day long, till the shades lengthen, and the evening comes, and the busy world is hushed, and the fever of life is over, and our work is done! Then in His mercy may He give us a safe lodging, and a holy rest, and peace at the last! (*S. S. D.*, p. 307)

INDEX